S.H.A.M.E!

SEXUAL HARASSMENT AGAINST MALES (BY FEMALES) EXPOSED

Martin & Deidre Bobgan

S.H.A.M.E! Sexual Harassment Against Males (By Females) Exposed

Copyright © 2020 Martin and Deidre Bobgan
Published by EastGate Publishers
4137 Primavera Road
Santa Barbara, CA 93110

Library of Congress Control Number:2020945785
ISBN 978-0941717-29-8

S.H.A.M.E! is written in support of:

- Moral men who do not want to be distracted or harassed by sexy-looking females.

- Women who have been sexually objectified without their knowledge or will.

- Girls and boys who are being harmed by an overly sexualized culture.

- Women who will choose to make a difference by what they wear.

Table of Contents

1

Sexual Harassment Against Males (By Females) Exposed

S.H.A.M.E! Sexual Harassment Against Males[1] *(By Females*[2]*) Exposed!* is about the sexual impact on males of sexually provocative female practices and presentations that are overt and in plain sight to males, but hidden in plain sight, overtly overlooked, and ignominiously ignored by females. As we will demonstrate, males are regularly and routinely the objects of sexual harassment by the female gender every day and in many worrisome ways. We document the who, what, when, where, why, and how this sexual harassment against males by females occurs and what females need to do to stop sexually harassing males.

Numerous volumes have been written on the history of the public undressing of women. Some have surmised that it all began in a woman's bedroom with the underclothing of a bra and girdle. Some of the chroniclers of fashion say that female fashions first migrated from the bedroom to the beach. At the beach the women's swimsuits obviously evolved from barely any skin showing to revealing more nudity inch by inch. All agree that Hollywood, through its movies, was a major influence in the early denuding of the female body, followed by television, and all the other media and print portrayals. Many sources concurrently set the standards for the female fashion freedoms. It is not our intention to trace the entire history of the public undressing of females. Instead, we will describe what current female fashions are worn by females who are sexually harassing males and leave the extensive historical panorama that preceded the present parade of pulchritude to others.

Later we will introduce a second S.H.A.M.E! acronym for Sexual **Harm** Against **Minors** Exposed and explain the connection between the two acronyms. Finally, we will introduce a third S.H.A.M.E! acronym for Sexual Harassment Against Males (By Females) **Ended**! The first two acronyms are essential to understanding how a large section of the male population, including both men and boys, are affected by the splendiferous sexy bodies that many women and girls flash in public.

#MeToo

The popularized MeToo movement has effectively opened eyes to much of the sexual harm perpetrated against females by males. Such sexual harm against females, hidden away through intimidation and fear, is now in view and the view is getting sharper as one female after another speaks out about what males did to them behind closed doors. **This book is about what females do to males in plain sight.**

The following describes the MeToo movement and how it spread:

The **MeToo movement** (or **#MeToo movement**), with a large variety of local and international related names, is a movement against sexual harassment and sexual assault. The movement began to spread virally in October 2017 as a hashtag on social media in an attempt to demonstrate the widespread prevalence of sexual assault and harassment, especially in the workplace.[3]

The #MeToo movement is a valuable and viable one to reveal what has been hidden in plain sight for many years, i.e., overt and covert "sexual harassment and sexual assault" of women by men. It was a long time in coming and we commend all those women who came forward and exposed all those men who were outed as a result. Any male who moves to offensively commenting, ogling, touching, or, God forbid, doing anything more deserves condemnation and referral to the law if deserved.

Males who cross the line are one hundred percent guilty; but, **so too are the females who, naively or not, become sexual provocateurs**. Many of the reported #MeToo offences against females are physically and emotionally serious. The *S.H.A.M.E!* offenses against males are emotionally, ethically, and, for many, even morally harmful to them. Even though the male sexual response is different from a female sexual response, the same moral and ethical standards must apply to both genders or not at all. The standard we are using is:

Harassment occurs where there is unwanted conduct on the ground of a person's sex or unwanted conduct of a sexual nature and that conduct has the purpose or effect of violating a person's dignity, or of creating an intimidating, hostile, degrading, humiliating or offensive environment for them.[4]

As a hoped-for result of this book, we propose a new movement to end this widespread Sexual Harassment Against Males (By Females). We ask that, as a result of reading this book, males will rapidly and readily come forward and air their complaints and the females who are guilty will be exposed, admit their guilt, realize the personal damage they have done, and halt the harassment. And, as a result of reading this book, females will readily come forward to air their complaints about those females who are guilty of harassing males.

Words in the Title of *S.H.A.M.E!*

What do we mean by the compelling acronym in the title *S.H.A.M.E!*? To clarify how and why we use such a strong acronym, we will describe each word and phrase.

Sexual

The adjective *sexual* is defined as "relating to the instincts, physiological processes, and activities connected with physical attraction or intimate physical contact between individuals."[5] We are **not** referring to "intimate, physical contact between individuals," which was the sexual abuse subject of the #MeToo movement. Instead, we will reveal how "the **instincts**, physiological processes, and activities connected with physical attraction" lead to the sexual harassment against males by **sexy females**. Significantly, *sexual instinct* is "the innate drive to have **sexual** relations. In biological terms

instincts are behaviors that occur as if natural and without teaching or model. They are species-specific practices for life and survival."[6] The adjective *sexy*, as in "sexy females," is defined as "sexually suggestive or stimulating: erotic."[7] *Sexy* can also mean "seductive."

Harassment

In addition to the standard quoted above, we use the following definition for *harassment*: "Harassment is unwanted, unwelcomed and uninvited behavior that demeans… or offends the victim and results in a hostile environment for the victim."[8] The kind of harassment this book addresses is not an overt (obvious) harassment, but rather a covert (hidden in plain sight) harassment, not willingly admitted by the guilty females involved. In fact, it is often vehemently denied and blamed on the male mentality.

Against

The definition of *against* is "in opposition to." As sexual harassment by males against females is in opposition to their desires and boundaries, so also sexual harassment by females against males is in opposition to their desires and boundaries.

Males (By Females)

The males to whom we refer are continually subjected to "unwanted, unwelcomed and uninvited behavior that demeans… [and] offends the victim and results in a hostile environment for the victim."[9] The behavior of certain females will demean and offend these males if they are trapped into having to observe them. Such an environment becomes internally threatening if there is no way of escaping the sight of a female's sexually provocative presence. These males will feel like victims experiencing a "hostile environment."

Exposed

The word *exposed* means "not covered or hidden, visible."[10] In *S.H.A.M.E!* we are exposing what has been hidden in plain sight to many females. We will give visibility to what may be hidden to females, but in glaringly plain sight to males.

The reason we are using the male and female genders in addition to the terms *men* and *women* is because this hidden-in-plain-sight sexual harassment of males also exists against boys by girls. Sexual harassment by females begins before girls are women, and those harassed include boys as well as men, as we reveal later.

Females and Males

Females

Some females are aware of how the visual impact of their exposed body parts affects males and knowingly dress in revealing ways. Some make a generous living off those males who enjoy the erotic entertainment. However, such female bodily exposures are harassing those males who desire to avoid seeing such bodily sights. The sexually offending females are obstacles to those males who want to regard females as fellow travelers together on the road of life. Those females who make themselves sexually enticing by their exposed or partially exposed body parts end up being seen for what they are: sex objects! Moreover, they lead the way for males to regard all females as sex objects.

There are other females who are unaware of their bodily sexual impact on males and are naïve or innocent of knowingly doing it. However, once informed, they should take the responsibility and dress modestly. The numerous females who become knowledgeable about the sexual impact of their body parts on males and do not change are doubly guilty of sexual harassment against males. First, when they do it innocently and, second, when they knowingly and purposefully display their bodies for their sexual appeal. We hope that the many females who are not aware of the sexual impact of their bodies on males will read this book and reform for the sake of both men and boys and even for themselves, as we will explain later.

On the other hand, a multitude of females will agree with much of what *S.H.A.M.E!* stands for and with what we are saying. **These females will immediately understand our plea to their fellow females** and come alongside our efforts to effect change. **These are moral females as to their stand on this subject.** The definition of the adjective *moral* that we are using is "concerned with or relating to human behavior, especially the distinction between good and bad or right and wrong... adhering to conventionally accepted standards based on a sense of right and wrong according to conscience." *Morals* (noun) are standards of right and wrong, that individuals and groups determine. Later, we will describe "moral feminists."

Males

Because the United states is made up of people from many parts of the world, numerous religions are represented. However, the three largest groups are Christianity, Judaism, and Islam. But not all Americans follow a defined faith system and many are of "no religion." Thus, there is no single standard of morality that everyone follows. However, because we are dealing with the **limited subject of the sexualization of females and its numerous effects, we are using the words *moral males* as they apply in this single area of morality**. In doing so, we are not generalizing the moniker *moral males* to other areas of life. Within this limited context, we define *moral males* as those males who choose to conduct themselves according to a standard of right and wrong in the area of sexual behavior. This book is about the moral males who find themselves in an awkward, uncomfortable, genitally challenging position (described later) when confronted by uninvited female bodily exposure. These harassed males will resist, resent, and avoid being turned on sexually when confronted with the sexually provocative females.

We articulate the systemic sexual harassment of all those males who want to avoid being confronted by those females who are publicly displaying their bodies in sexually provocative ways. We further demonstrate how such female bodily exposure is harmful to men and boys and also harmful to women and girls, as we will explain later. When the males are sexually harassed, the females are objectified in the transaction, and society is overly sexualized. The males who need protection from female harassment are those who want to avoid being sexually aroused by the display of certain female body parts.

Besides the harassed males, there are other males who enjoy looking at the many sexy female bodies on display. We call the males who willingly submit to their desires to look at sexy females "indulgers." An *indulger* within this context is a male who indulges himself sexually; that is, he chooses to enjoy the sensual pleasure sexy-looking females provide for him. However, we do not want to leave the impression that the indulgers lack of moral restraint in this one area necessarily reveals an overall lack of character. An indulger may begin simply by paying extra attention and enjoying the satisfaction of being sexually stimulated. Indulgers may enjoy the sensual scenery in an almost casual way, but too many indulgers like the satisfaction so much that their lust drives them into pornography. No one knows how many of those males have been thus tempted through the sexy females they see each day. Naive females would never think or imagine that their own sexual appeal through apparel or lack thereof may be a beginning stimulus for a male to just peak at porn.

Males who do not wish to be harassed by the un-avoidable presence of sexually stimulating females will avoid as much as possible the normal mental and physical response by refraining, as much as possible, from view-ing the sexy females who are on parade each day. Those moral males we are writing about are the ones who are sexually harassed by females, because such display can arouse a built-in male genital response (described later) that conflicts with their moral standards. These males will experience harassment when being confronted by females provocatively or partially dressed. They feel harassed under such circumstances, because they must exercise mental effort to resist by suppressing their thinking away from the natural sexual thoughts that have been stimulated by unavoidably seeing sexy-looking females.

Females as Whole Persons

Moral males are offended by female sexual display. They desire to respect females as mothers, sisters, wives and fellow human beings traveling through life's joys and difficulties. However, this desire to respect females as equals is challenged by those females who immodestly display their bodies. In contrast, by dressing modestly, females have the capacity to remove the burden from the males who want to regard them as fellow human beings with qualities of personhood, intelligence, and ability.

These harassed males want to see a female as a whole person—an equal human being—not their exposed and erotic sexy parts. Female bodily exposure and/or exaggeration will serve as obstacles to males who would rather see women as individuals with abilities, personality, and virtues. Yes, moral males are often forced to look at sexy females, even though they would prefer not to and dislike the effect when such exposure cannot be avoided. With so many sexy-looking female body parts within eyesight every day, it is hard not to look, even with the best of intentions. That's harassment!

The harassed males we are defending are those who not only desire to see females as whole persons, but also to treat them with respect as equal human beings. However, females whose bodies are sexually displayed will challenge that desire and commitment. They interrupt a male's intention to regard them in the manner that most woman would want—equality. It is very difficult for a male to get past the displayed sexually-enticing body parts to see and appreciate the individual herself. By dressing modestly, females can avoid challenging a male's genitals and help prevent him from **objectifying** her as a collection of sexually-stimulating body parts. One bottom-line goal is for males and females to respect and value each other as complete human beings—as amazing compositions of body, mind, and soul/spirit, all of which work together to make each person a unique individual.

Not Recommending Extremes

Although we are not recommending such extreme forms of hiding the female body as in the following examples, we include them here **as a contrast and to illustrate how harassing provocative female exposure can be to certain males**. The following two examples are from groups that have strict standards for female modesty. The first example is "extreme ultra-Orthodox Jewish men who shun contact with the opposite sex" and wear blurry glasses to avoid seeing women whom they consider immodestly dressed.[11] The second example is the Hijab, which represents the Islamic clothing standard:

> The Arabic word *hijab* translates into English as "veil." Adherents of Islam believe that it is a command by God to adult Muslim men and women, carrying the ruling of obligatory, which is agreed upon by consensus. In addition, lowering the gaze and guarding one's chastity stand as vital aspects of wearing the hijab....

According to the traditional view in Sunni Islam, women must cover everything except their hands and faces, and their feet may be exposed in the Hanafi school.[12]

In giving the above two examples we want to make it clear that we are not recommending blurry glasses. **We are definitely not recommending or even suggesting female shrouding or extreme clothing restrictions for females.**

Modesty does not have to be extreme. A good example of modesty is described in the current understanding of the Jewish *tznuit*:

> The principal guiding point of *tzniut* in regard to dress is that a Jew should not dress in a way that attracts undue attention. This does not mean dressing poorly, but that neither men nor women should dress in a way that overly emphasizes their physical appearance or attracts undue attention.[13]

This is a standard that all moral males, moral females, and moral feminists (described later) would agree needs to be followed. Many of the moral males who are harassed belong to a faith system and desire to hold to the standards of their faith in thought and behavior.

Gender Differences

There are great similarities between males and females; yet, there are some significant differences that affect their sexual views of one another. It seems trivial and almost unnecessary to say this, but males and females are different from one another, and these differences enter into how they perceive one another as sexual beings. In addition to sexual differences between males and females, there are biological, behavioral, hormonal, and functional differences, which factor into these differences.

Differences between males and females begin before birth and continue throughout life. *Science News* reports:

> The reason boys like trucks and girls like dolls relates to fetal differences in brain development, explains Heather Patisaul, a neuroendrocrinologist at North Carolina State University in Raleigh. Males develop differently from females— physically and behaviorally—largely through programming by androgens (male sex hormones such as testosterone).[14]

The *Scientific American Mind* reports in "The Neural Roots of Intelligence" on the differences in the neural networks of intelligence in men and women. They say:

> The specific areas in this network are different in men and women, suggesting there are at least two different brain architectures that produce equivalent performance on IQ tests. In general, we found that in women more gray and white matter in frontal brain areas, especially those associated with language, was correlated with IQ scores; in men IQ scores correlated with gray matter in frontal areas and, especially, in posterior areas that integrate sensory information.[15]

Of course, there are similarities between the brains of males and females. However, *Scientific American* says, "It turns out that male and female brains differ quite a bit in architecture and activity." The journal also says that "over the past decade investigators have documented an astonishing array of structural, chemical and functional variations in the brains of males and females."[16] The *Scientific American Mind* produced a special issue devoted to "Male vs. Female Brains" with the words "His Brain, Her Brain, How we're different" on the cover.[17] While this special issue does speak of similarities between the sexes, it is primarily about the differences. One writer sums it up by saying: "There is ample evidence that men and women think, express themselves and even experience emotions differently."[18]

Linguist Deborah Tannen explains "Genderspeak" as follows: "Men's talk tends to focus on hierarchy—competition for relative power—whereas women's [talk] tends to focus on connection—relative closeness or distance."[19] The differences in the brains of males and females influence how they perceive and act. There are many other gender differences, but we offer only a few more in the following paragraphs.

One group of researchers reveals the following:

> Beauty is in the brain of the beholder. Go to any museum and there will be men and women admiring paintings and sculpture. But it turns out they are thinking about the sight differently. Men process beauty on the right side of their brains, while women use their whole brain to do the job, researchers report in Tuesday's electronic edition of Proceedings of the National Academy of Science. They even explain it differently....

Researchers were surprised by the finding. "It is well known that there are differences between brain activity in women and men in cognitive tasks," said researcher Camilo J. Cela-Conde of the University of Baleares in Palma de Mallorca, Spain. "However, why should this kind of difference appear in the case of appreciation of beauty?" The answer seems to be that when women consider a visual object they link it to language while men concentrate on the spatial aspects of the object.[20]

A *Scientific American* article titled "Taking Sex Differences in Personality Seriously" reveals that "New approaches are shedding light on the magnitude of sex differences in personality, and the results are so strong and pervasive that they can no longer be ignored." The article says, "*On average,* males tend to be more dominant, assertive, risk-prone, thrill-seeking, tough-minded, emotionally stable, utilitarian, and open to abstract ideas…. In contrast, females, *on average*, tend to be more sociable, sensitive, warm, compassionate, polite, anxious, self-doubting, and more open to aesthetics." After considering the research, the author declares that "in recent years it's becoming increasingly clear that when you take a look at the overall *gestalt* of personality—taking into account the correlation between the traits—the differences between the sexes become all the more striking"[20] (italics in original).

Dr. James W. Pennebaker of the University of Texas at Austin and his colleagues have "developed a computer program that analyzes texts called Linguistic Inquiry and Word Count (LIWC, pronounced 'Luke')."[22] Through the use of LIWC, Pennebaker et al. reveal by statistical analysis that "the way we write and speak can reveal volumes about our identity and character." They say, "In general, women tend to use more pronouns and references to other people. Men are more likely to use articles, prepositions and big words."[23] This certainly affects in cross-gender perceptions of sex.

According to some theories, men in general are "better at systemizing" and "women are better at empathizing."[24] Here, too, these differences affect sexual views of one gender to another. Females do what they do so well—being verbal, nurturing, and relational. Females tend to share, communicate, and converse, which is why psychotherapy is becoming more and more predominantly a female profession with the clients primarily being females.[25]

Illuminating What Is Hidden in Plain Sight

The message of this book is actually to the advantage of both males and females as we attempt to illuminate what is hidden in plain sight. The women and girls who see what is in plain sight will recognize that what we say is to their advantage as well as to the advantage of moral men and boys. We want to emphasize that, although females are not the cause of what males do after they are sexually stimulated by what they see, women are responsible for the sexual stimulation they provide when they seductively display their bodies. **A later chapter will help reveal more clearly what is hidden in plain sight, as we look at the instant neural communication from male eyes to the mind and genitals.**

2

Precursors of the Public Undressing of Females

Sexual modesty was the original reason for covering up. We see this in the beginning of the Bible, where Adam and Eve realized their nakedness and "they sewed fig leaves together and made themselves aprons" (Genesis 3:7). Females have come a long way from the Garden of Eden story to the current bodily display.

The sexual revolution preceded the current undressing of women. According to Wikipedia:

> The **sexual revolution**, also known as a time of **sexual liberation**, was a social movement that challenged traditional codes of behavior related to sexuality and interpersonal relationships throughout the United States and subsequently, the wider world, from the 1960s to the 1980s.[1]

In addition, Wikipedia describes the women's liberation movement as follows:

> The **women's liberation movement (WLM)** was a political alignment of women and feminist intellectualism that emerged in the late 1960s

and continued into the 1980s primarily in the industrialized nations of the Western world, which effected great change (political, intellectual, cultural) throughout the world.[2]

The sexual revolution was a catalyst for the women's liberation movement, which began later but ran concomitant with it. The sexual revolution could well have been named "the sexual liberation movement." Once "traditional codes of behavior related to sexuality and interpersonal relationships" were challenged, the door for the women's liberation movement sprang wide open. The sexual revolution was a cry for sexual equality on the part of women and a desire to overcome being a subordinate class. The women's liberation movement demanded change in the political, intellectual, cultural, and sexual areas of life and a cessation of second-class status.

The sexual revolution and the women's liberation movement of the 1960s through the 1980s dramatically challenged much of the culturally embedded discrimination against women. There were legitimate and needed challenges to the political, intellectual, and cultural status quo regarding women. There were necessary changes regarding equality that the women's liberation movement has encouraged and supported regarding the treatment of women. In fact, this book highlights an area of exploitation of women which reduces their worth as equal individuals with men by enticing them to being sex objects. This is done through displaying sexually enticing female bodies, which actually puts women in a one-down position as they are naively or knowingly inviting the kind of attention that actually reduces them to sex objects—

just the very opposite of what the early pioneers of the women's liberation movement had in mind.

Influence of Affluence

The sexual revolution and the women's liberation movement of the 60s through the 80s could not have occurred during the ten-year period of the depression, which began in 1929. One of the most important ingredients in the sexual revolution is affluence. With increasing affluence, individuals focused more on self-fulfillment and personal satisfaction. The prevailing idea was that, if each person is fulfilled and satisfied, society's ills would be healed. It was apparent that, in order for this to happen, many of the historic customs of the past regarding equal opportunities and treatment needed to be accorded to women.

Influence of Secular Humanism

In her book *Road to Malpsychia*, Joyce Milton notes:

> By the 1960s the stage was set for a radically simplified view of human nature, influenced by existentialism but with a unique American spin. To maximize one's potential, one had to throw off the distorting influences of society and discover and nurture one's innate good self.[3]

Humanistic psychology paved the way for a new concept of the self that needed to be freed from the restraints of "repressive social institutions and moral codes" so that people would be "free to develop their inborn goodness" and "build a society without hypocrisy, prejudice or exploitation."[4]

But even before the development of humanistic psychology, Sigmund Freud (1856-1939), considered the father of the psychotherapy movement, believed that morality, particularly sexual morality, was at the root of psychological disorders. Indeed Freud's influence is such that E.M. Thornton in *The Freudian Fallacy* declares:

> Probably no single individual has had a more profound effect on twentieth-century thought than Sigmund Freud. His works have influenced psychiatry, anthropology, social work, penology, and education and provided a seemingly limitless source of material for novelists and dramatists. Freud has created a "whole new climate of opinion"; for better or worse he has changed the face of society.[5]

Abraham Maslow (1908-1970) followed many of Freud's ideas regarding sexual freedom and belief in a powerful unconscious that motivates behavior. Maslow, considered by many to be one of the founders of humanistic psychology, contended that people are innately good and possess "innate instincts" within themselves to enable them to find values within the self rather than looking to an outside source.[6]

The Media: Public Proclamation of Change

Of course, the sexual revolution was only the beginning. The leaven of the sexual revolution and the women's liberation movement continued to expand both through advocacy groups and the media. The world entered every life, not just through the ears (radio), but through the eyes (television, print, and media). The women's liberation movement worked for the removal of the political, intellectual, cultural, and all restraining barriers in all areas of life that prevent women from gaining full equality with men. It was through the influence of affluence and the liberation movements that women were free to think about what to wear.

Communication of Clothing

William Shakespeare's oft-quoted words "The apparel oft proclaims the man" form a truism that began in ancient times and continues right up today. The color of the dancer's costume in the ballet *Swan Lake* communicates whether the ballerina is Odette, the true swan, or Odile, her evil opponent, even as the same ballerina dances both parts. Odette is in glistening white; Odile is in stunning black. Color, style, fabric, and design often say more than words can express.

What people wear can tell the viewer what might be a special occasion or a destination. One outfit may reveal an intended trip to a concert, a back-packing trek, a particular profession, or just hanging out. Not only can dress differ according to place and event, but clothing can reveal aspects of personality and character and also what is in fashion. Allison Lurie begins her book *The Language of Clothes* by saying:

> For thousands of years human beings have communicated with one another first in the language of dress. Long before I am near enough to talk to you on the street, in a meeting or at a party, you announce your sex, age, and class to me through what you are wearing—and very possibly give

me important information (or misinformation)
as to your occupation, origin, personality opin-
ions, tastes, sexual desires and current mood. I
may not be able to put what I observe into words,
but I register the information unconsciously; and
you simultaneously do the same for me. By the
time we meet and converse we have already spo-
ken to each other in an older and more universal
tongue.[7]

In her chapter "Male and Female," Lurie says:

Some modern writers believe that the deliberate
concealment of certain parts of the body originat-
ed not as a way of discouraging sexual interest,
but as a clever device for arousing it. According
to this view, clothes are the physical equivalent
of remarks like "I've got a secret"; they are a
tease, a come-on. It is certainly true that parts of
the human form considered sexually arousing are
often covered in such a way as to emphasize and
draw attention to them.[8]

Later she says:

Whether it was the first cause or not, from the
earliest times one important function of clothing has been to promote erotic activity: to attract
men and women to one another, thus ensuring the
survival of the species. If maximum fertility is
to be achieved, we must select members of the
opposite sex rather than our own to make love
to. One basic purpose of costume, therefore, is to
distinguish men from women.[9]

In her book *What We Wore*, Ellen Melinkoff describes how fashions displayed on television influenced women's fashion preferences from the 1950s to the 1980s:

> TV opened up the world to us, including the fashion of the world. It let us see what people were wearing with an intensity, and immediacy we had never had. Before that time, we relied on *LIFE*, fashion magazines, and movies for guidance. But those media were remote and told us what a model or movie star had worn months ago.[10]

But that was back then and the possibilities, even beyond movies and television, are everywhere on social media such as Instagram, with all kinds of visual possibilities for what to wear.

The Undressing of American Females

Today more females appear partially clad or immodestly exposed in public than during any other period of history in the United States. This increase in bodily exposure is due mostly to the media and to the World Wide Web, which was born August 6, 1991.[11] Such flagrant exposure puts unwanted pressure on those moral males who do not want to be titillated by females exposing themselves publicly. They feel harassed because the absence of clothing violates their religious or ethical reservations. They do not want to be sexually stimulated by the exposure of nakedness by females who are either naively or knowingly flaunting their bodies. Throughout every day, moral males are constantly hammered by the non-stop display of sexually harassing females. This book is written for the many males who feel harassed by what they are forced to see almost everywhere they go. And, it is written for the females who are harassing these males, so they may see the personal damage that may occur and also avoid what appears to those who wish to avoid the male gaze that sees women as sex objects. The male gaze "presents and represents women as sexual objects for the pleasure of the male viewer."[12]

Beaches

The public undressing of America began at the beach and exploded through the influence of Hollywood, television, the media, and the fashion industry. On the front cover of the book *Making Waves*, the subtitle describes the book's contents: *Swimsuits and the Undressing of America*. The first two paragraphs are an exciting beginning to an exciting-to-read book.

> The history of the American swimsuit is the square-inch-by-square-inch story of how skin went public in modern times. In an equally important sense, it is also the story of how flesh and fabric have come together to serve sport, sex, and culture.

> The unexpurgated—and oftentimes steamy— saga of this classical garment can be seen as a tug of war between skin, machine, and cloth choreographed by the forces of concealment and disclosure, and performed against the shifting sands of civilization and its discontents.[13]

The authors go on to say:

Clothing is erotic because it arouses curiosity about the body as a whole. Seen in this light, the swimsuit has functioned as a kind of sartorial italics that, over time, have been refocusing erotic attention on various parts of the human body.

In *Splash!: The History of Swimwear*, the authors reveal the significant role that Hollywood has played in the undressing of both the female and male body. They say and substantiate that: "Hollywood realized that though movies could talk, few conversations equaled the unutterable sex appeal of cinema flesh." The authors say and support the fact that "Fashion magazines contributed substantially to the evolution of women's swimwear of the period.... Most importantly, fashion magazines wrought their characteristic transformation on women's swimwear; they created icons and a visual system." [14]

A look at any active beach in America will reveal what constitutes show time for female bodies. A number of books document the early swimming attire and the evolution of swim suits to the present-day styles of female beach wear that expose female body parts to limits near nakedness. The chronology of body parts covered to body parts revealed is an interesting story in itself. However, the important point in our investigation is that the book places the primary influence of Americans following female beachwear fashions of Hollywood, next television, and eventually all media together with the fashion industry as they capitalize on "sex sells."

Sex Sells

Advertisers use sex appeal to help sell products or services. Sexually appealing imagery most often includes female nudity or partial nudity. The greater the titillation, the greater the attention-grabbing effect on potential male buyers. Note how many ads include a female figure that is well-defined and often provocative—not only to capture the gaze, but to hold the attention and set a connection between the female and the merchandise.

Entire books have been written about sex in advertising. The use of sexual imagery to attract sales is so ubiquitous that no one would even question its use. A *Business News Daily* article, entitled "Why Sex Sells... More than Ever," reports:

> Advertisers use sexual imagery to attract sales of products as diverse as perfume and cheeseburgers. While using sexy ads might seem like a risky choice, studies show that it works. Sex sells because it immediately grabs attention....
>
> Tom Reichert, a professor and head of the Department of Advertising and Public Relations at the University of Georgia Grady College of Journalism and Mass Communication [states], "Sex sells because it attracts attention. People are hardwired to notice sexually relevant information, so ads with sexual content get noticed."
>
> Reichert said this upward trend in erotic ads is a reflection of society. "It takes more explicitness to grab our attention and arouse us than before," he said. "In the early 1900s, exposed arms and ankles of female models generated the same level of arousal as partially nude models do today. We can see during our lifetimes the changes in sexually explicit content on television, movies,

books and other forms of media beyond just advertising."[15]

Yes, "sex sells," but, *sexy* sells too. We repeat, the adjective *sexy*, as in "sexy females," is defined as "sexually suggestive or stimulating: erotic."[16] *Sexy* can also mean "seductive." For males, *sexy* equates to being sexually stimulated by a female body dressed, partially dressed, or undressed in a manner that elicits sexual arousal. For females, *sexy* means to be cute, personally attractive, exciting, or appealing. "Sex sells." But, so does *sexy* for many females who naively reveal sexually stimulating parts of the body that males will see as sexual and react bodily.

All the while, these naive females think they are only being stylishly sexy and thereby strive to look sexy, not realizing that they are actually turning themselves into sex objects in the eyes of males. Such a female is not even considering the possibility of a male viewer being aroused and thinking about SEX. In fact, the very idea that any male who looks at her might be genitally aroused by her sexy apparel or manner would be offensive to her! She would blame him for being sexually stimulated in the first place. Although she may think she is simply looking stylishly sexy, a male's bodily responses will be evident to him in his mind (thinking) and body (genitals).

The moral male who recognizes his bodily proclivities and wishes to avoid the mind/body challenge will, nevertheless, be sexually aroused if exposed to the many females who are partly undressed and/or emphasize certain body parts in public. These teasingly clad or partly unclad, sexually provocative females are seen by moral males, who are forced to see what they prefer not to see. Such harassed males will unwillingly be moved up the ladder of sexual arousal.

Many articles **critically expose** what many females have already exposed: their bodies! Such articles are generally regarded as oppressive, body shaming, or victim blaming. However, the male response to visual enticement is biologically driven—**involuntary**—as we shall show. In contrast, the female desire to look sexy is **voluntary**! The definition of *voluntary* is "acting according to one's free will." In contrast, the definition of *involuntary* is "done without will or conscious control." **The female has a choice, the male does not!** All the more reason why *Sexual Harassment Against Males (By Females)* [must be] *Exposed.*

Before describing the appearance of those females who sexually harass males, we describe what we are not including. If one goes on an internet search and types in the word *sexy* followed by any visible body part, one will find a plethora of possibilities. Try *sexy toes, toenails, feet, ankles, calves, thighs, hands, arms, elbows, shoulders,* etc. We are not speaking about those individual body parts as being guilty of causing a testosterone response in males who ingest the view. Males looking at a woman will not usually be sexually harassed by any of the above-mentioned body parts, because they are generally not sexually arousing. In contrast, an indulger might think and fantasize fellacio by merely seeing a woman's lips. We are not coming to the defense of such individuals.

In addition, if one does an internet search of "What makes a woman sexy?" one will find *sexy* defined with numerous words, such as: *confident, ambitious, kind, honest, intelligent, smiles, magnetic, fun, independent, has integrity, vulnerable, open, feminine, nurturing*, etc. However, these fall under the categories of behavior, character, or personality. These are the qualities or virtues that a male can experience, describe, and appreciate in a female without being genitally disturbed. But, in spite of what the various internet entries claim, the above personal aspects of females would not, in themselves, be sexually arousing, and therefore they would not fall into the category of titillating the "indulgers" or harassing the moral males.

A female can act in a variety of ways. Prostitutes know how to ply their trade by use of their partially clad bodies, which invite a desire to see more and do more. The males who would be harassed by such obvious displays of sexual enticement and entrapment would rather avoid them. The closer a female's dress looks like a prostitute's, the greater the possibility for harassment. Moral males will recognize such fleshly appeals and resist being lured into their moral undoing.

3

The Eyes Have It

The eyes are the focus of *S.H.A.M.E!* The nervous system of the body has five traditionally recognized senses: seeing (eyes), hearing (ears), tasting (mouth), smelling (nose), and touching (skin). Although the other four senses can all be used by a woman to be attractive to a man, the eyes are the primary sense organs that *S.H.A.M.E!* centers on, through females who sexually harass males.

EurekAlert Science News reports, "The Eyes Have It: Men do see things differently to women." A study of the brain reveals:

> The way that the visual centers of men and women's brains works is different, finds new research published in BioMed Central's open access journal *Biology of Sex Differences.* Men have greater sensitivity to fine detail and rapidly moving stimuli but women are better at discriminating between colors. [1]

An article from *ScienceDaily* says much the same thing: "It's all in the eyes: Women and men really do see things differently." The Summary of the article reveals:

Women and men look at faces and absorb visual information in different ways, which suggests there is a gender difference in understanding visual cues, according to a team of scientists that included psychologists from Queen Mary University of London.[2]

The key words here are: "there is a gender difference in understanding visual cues." The *Journal of Sexual Medicine* reports on a study that reveals that it is the woman's body and not the man's body that is used to evaluate sexual desire. Their subtitle reveals the method used in this research: "An Eye-Tracking Study of Automatic Visual Attention." The word "automatic" is quite telling. The authors begin by saying, "Vision of the human body has been shown to be key in eliciting sexual desire." Their conclusion states: "These findings confirm the association between the human body and sexual desire. They also reveal the unique attentional attractiveness of women's bodies across genders."[3]

As we shall demonstrate in this chapter, when a male sees a sexy-looking female, he can be literally turned on, **whether he wants to be or not**. The difference between how males see females and how females see males is something many women do not seem to realize, know, or understand. And, it's not just **how** males see females, but **what the seeing certain sexy females does to them**.

Hard-Wired

Hard-wired is defined as "pertaining to or being an intrinsic and relatively unmodifiable behavior pattern."[4] How is the brain hard-wired?

The brain is hard-wired with connections, much like a skyscraper or airplane is hard-wired with electrical wiring. In the case of the brain, the connections are made by neurons that link the sensory inputs and motor outputs with centers in the various lobes of the cerebral cortex.[5]

Some of the hard-wiring has to do with emotions. According to James Madison University, "You are born with these emotions wired into your brain. That wiring causes your body to react in certain ways and for you to have certain urges when the emotion arises." They list the following as being "wired into your brain":

- Anger: fury, outrage, wrath, irritability, hostility, resentment and violence.

- Sadness: grief, sorrow, gloom, melancholy, despair, loneliness, and depression.

- Fear: anxiety, apprehension, nervousness, dread, fright, and panic.

- Joy: enjoyment, happiness, relief, bliss, delight, pride, thrill, and ecstasy.

- Interest: acceptance, friendliness, trust, kindness, affection, love, and devotion.

- Surprise: shock, astonishment, amazement, astound, and wonder.

- Disgust: contempt, disdain, scorn, aversion, distaste, and revulsion.

•Shame: guilt, embarrassment, chagrin, remorse, regret, and contrition.[6]

Using *fear* as an example of hardwiring, one website reveals:

> Research suggests that information about potentially frightening things in the environment can reach the amygdala before we are even consciously aware that there's anything to be afraid of. There is a pathway that runs from the thalamus to the amygdala, and sensory information about fearful stimuli may be sent along this pathway to the amygdala before it is consciously processed by the cerebral cortex. This allows for the initiation of a fear reaction before we even have time to think about what it is that's so frightening.[7]

In addition to the emotions being hard-wired, other hard-wiring has to do with bodily responses to environmental cues, such as a hunger response to the aroma of freshly baked bread. Or, the adrenalin rush accompanying anger or joy. Or the quick physical response when touching a scalding hot surface. This chapter deals with a male's hard-wired bodily response to certain visual stimuli.

The Male Brain

The hormone testosterone plays a large part in every man's life, and it has been revealed that during puberty "testosterone floods his whole organism."[8] Between ages nine and eighteen a boy's testosterone levels dramatically increase until they peak at about age 20.[9] From then on this powerful hormone biologically masculinizes a male's thoughts and behaviors, which originate in his brain, some of which often precede his conscious awareness. Female sexy body parts then become visual signals that light up the male brain with lightning speed. A man's genitals instinctively respond to a sexy female, sometimes even before he is fully conscious of her. Reason enough for the moral males who know this and do not want to be there with a female body glaring them in the face and affecting their genitals.

When observing sexy females, unconscious signals from a man's spinal cord and brain can cause a spontaneous erection. Females need to know that the penis can operate spontaneously and become erect even though men do not always know it is happening. During the years that males have the highest testosterone levels, focusing on a hot, sexy female is all it takes for a man's penis to become fully erect.

Male brains are hard-wired to focus on and **objectify sexy females**. There is a certain formula all females need to be aware of, which is that the sexier you look, the more a male will objectify you in his mind (thoughts) and have a bodily response (genitals). Because of their biological make-up, males are not responsible for their automatic, instinctive bodily responses to sexual displays that females provide. Whether they know it or not, sexy-looking females are providing the fuel that inflames male genitals.

To reveal what happens when males view voluptuous females, let us first consider the word *instinct*, which is defined as "a natural or inherent aptitude, impulse or capacity," which is "a largely inheritable and unalterable tendency of an organism to make a complex and specific response to environmental stimuli without involving reason."[10] In applying the word *instinct* to humans, we see that:

> Like all animals, humans have instincts, genetically hard-wired behaviors that enhance our ability to cope with vital environmental contingencies. Our innate fear of snakes is an example.... Any attempt to control human behavior is bound to meet with resistance and disapproval.[11]

All humans have instincts that are "genetically hard-wired behaviors." These behaviors are *instinctive*: "unconscious or automatic."[12] Instinctive behaviors are spontaneous or without premeditation. When a male focuses on a voluptuous female, his instinctive response is an erection, whether he wants one or not. Indulgers like to pleasure themselves in daily looking at sexy females. However, moral males choose to abstain, which is only possible with difficulty in the current, public, female fashion climate.

The Hard-Wired Male Brain

We obtained several books that dealt with the visual effects of sexy females on male genitals, and all the books we read were unanimous on the subject of a male's hard-wired, instinctive response to seeing a sexy female.[13] One of the books is by Dr. Ronald Virag, a distinguished medical doctor.[14] Virag's book *Erection: The User's Guide* is detailed and comprehensive regarding male erections. Varig gives a number of detailed descriptions of an erection under different circumstances. One of the circumstances is a sexy-female-provoked or induced erection, which originates in the brain and travels to the penis. An example would be a common one, where a male sees a sexy female during his walk through the day. Virag says, "The vision of a whole body or part of it" or "simply catching the sight of a silhouette" can sometimes ignite or induce an erection. He further says:

> The stimuli, from the specific cerebral centers take the nerve paths of the spinal cord to the penis and further produce the erection. Once again, this starting off is not literally intentional [deliberate or intended], but the result of a psychological environment of hormones impregnated neurons and neurotransmitters fueling the desire of sexual realisation.[15]

In the case of male sexuality, the instinctual penis response leads to a desire for sexual realization. The verb *desire* is "a strong feeling of wanting to have something or wishing for something to happen…. Strong sexual feeling or appetite."[16] On the one hand, this "desire of sexual realization" in response to a sexy woman should not be unilaterally acted on. However, females must themselves realize that they may be dressing in such a manner as to stimulate an observing male's "desire of sexual realization." Even though she does not cause what he chooses to do with his strong desire, she does carry the responsibility for seeding that desire and for harassing moral males, who are bound to resist a further look.

The male response to seeing a sexy woman is a **reflex response**. We give three definitions to dramatize our point. **Reflex** is: (1) "an action that is performed as a response to a stimulus and without conscious thought"[17];

(2) "A **reflex**, or **reflex action**, is an involuntary and nearly instantaneous movement in response to a stimulus. A reflex is made possible by neural pathways called reflex arcs which can act on an impulse before that impulse reaches the brain" [18]; (3) "An innate, immediate involuntary action to a stimulus without prior conscious thought."[19]

The Book of Erections is a brief, but well written book with the subtitle, *The Penis: A User's Guide*. The author, Dr. Saskia Verhagen simply describes the erection this way: "An erection is like a **reflex**: an unconscious reaction....The muscular tissue in the penis is truly unique, specialized to fill with blood in response to an involuntary pathway, essentially an unconscious action like a **reflex**"[20] (bold added).

Verhagen describes various pathways for the resultant erection, including the visual, which is our primary concern. She says:

> Erections happen as a result of **relaxation** of the arteries and the spongy, muscular tissue in the penis. As these open up, the penis fills with blood which gets trapped there, and it thereby becomes hard. Compare this to the muscles we can use at will, such as flexing a bicep.... An erection has more in common with a **reflex**, an involuntary response, which makes it much harder to control or rely on.[21] (Bold added.)

Moral males continually have to suppress their natural genital reflex responses when confronted by sexy females. They do this by deflecting their eyes and diverting their thinking, which becomes an on-

going daily ritual. Females need to know that at times the penis has a mind of its own and will have an erection by instinct, unconsciously and spontaneously, without even a prior desire to have sex! Night time erections and sometimes daytime erections can appear with males barely knowing, at times, that they are getting an erection. Sometimes males who are loaded with testosterone will climax if they pay attention to a sexy female image and start fantasizing about her. Many indulgers desire to do just that.

Shaunti Feldhahn, in her book *For Women Only: What You Need to Know About the Inner Lives of Men*, presents the view of what we call the moral males, as expressed through surveys of more than 1600 men. She reveals that the result of her surveys "has been repeatedly tested and carefully validated with highly reliable evidence."[22] Feldhahn conducted a global survey followed by individual interviews of some of the men.

In discussing "The Visual Wiring of the Male Brain," Feldhahn says that "brain scientists note two separate but related compulsions stemming from male brain wiring that greatly impact men in today's culture."[23] The first compulsion is: "A Man Can't Not notice." The answer to the following survey question demonstrates the strength of that compulsion.:

> Imagine you are sitting alone in a train station and a woman with a great body walks in and stands in a nearby line. What is your reaction to the woman? (Choose one answer.)[24]

Here's how the men responded on the global survey:

The first fact is that a whopping 98 percent of men put their response to an eye-catching woman in "*can't not notice*" categories (only 2 percent were unaffected by a woman with a great body).[25]

The compulsion to look is clearly described in one of her individual surveys:

> One husband with a happy twenty-year marriage described a typical scenario: "My wife and I recently went out to dinner at a nice restaurant with some friends. The hostess was extremely attractive and was wearing formfitting clothes that showed off a great figure. For the rest of the night, it was impossible not to be aware that she was across the restaurant, walking around. Our group had a great time with our lovely wives, but I guarantee you that our wives didn't know that every man at that table was acutely aware of that woman's presence and was doing his utmost not to look in that direction."

> In other words, the nucleus accumbens of the male brain had lit up, the biological impulse to visually consume that image had been triggered, and all the men were exerting their will to force their thoughts and their eyes away.[26]

If these men at the table continued to look intently and fantasize, they would likely have an unintended erection at their dinner time.

The second compulsion is: "A Man Has a Mental Photo File of Sexual Images." Feldhahn asserts: "Images often arise without warning, even if the guy doesn't want them." The results of another survey question bear that out. To the statement and question: "Many men have a mental set of sensual images that rise up or can be conjured up in their minds. Does this apply to you?" she found:

> In total, 87 percent of men say these images pop up in their heads. When you break down the demographics, it is roughly the same across the board—whether men are old or young, happily married or single, religious or not.[27]

Feldhahn adequately portrays the struggles that occur every day for the male out in public. The sexy females seen and "recorded" become "filed away" for future recollections, which is exactly what the moral males want to avoid. The more the sexy images are indulged in by a male, the larger the image file becomes. Such images will often appear later and can even appear during husband-wife intimacy. Feldhahn devotes a full chapter to: "Why It's So Difficult for Him Not to Look and So Hard to Forget What He's Seen."[28]

The Females Have It—The Choice Is Theirs

Warning to sexy females: You may be causing males to have erections by providing fuel for indulgers to fantasize, which could lead to an orgasm! Moral males, who do not want this sexual stimulation, are being harassed because they must internally suppress their natural instinctive urges. They must put forth effort to avoid looking and ruminating. Because an erection is a natural male response to gazing at sexy females, the more females dress in a sexy manner, the more males will likely have an erection the longer they look, which is sometimes un-avoidable. Then, indulging in such visual exposure can further stimulate a male's desire for sexual fulfillment and even further stimulation from pornography.

A husband who is at the job all day with sexy females in view will surely have SEX on his mind when he comes home. Briefly, the sexier the females present themselves in public, the more the male viewers will desire sex, es-pecially those who indulge themselves by looking longer than necessary. As more females have made themselves sexier, the male demand for more sexual satisfaction has sky rocketed, leading to marital disagreements, extra-marital affairs, divorces, and pornography.

A Catholic mother wrote a letter to the Notre Dame University school newspaper, with which the moral males would agree. After sitting behind a group of girls in church with her four sons, she said:

> I was at Mass at the Basilica with my family. In front of us was a group of young women, all wearing very snug-fitting leggings and all wear-ing short-waisted tops (so that the lower body was uncovered except for the leggings). Some of them truly looked as though the leggings had been painted on them....

> I wonder why no one thinks it's strange that the fashion industry has caused women to voluntari-ly expose their nether regions in this way. I was ashamed for the young women at Mass. I thought of all the other men around and behind us who couldn't help but see their behinds....

I didn't want to see them—but they were un-avoidable. How much more difficult for young guys to ignore them.[29]

Unfortunately, many responses to the above appeal were in defense of women being entitled to wear what they want. After all, they believe the problem is with the young men, not the young women, who, after all, are simply exercising their rights by wearing what is in fashion.

We hope that we have demonstrated in this chapter that females have more choice than the males. Females can choose what to wear, whereas males do not choose the hard-wired, instinctive physical response to sex-loaded cues. Yes, the choice is up to the females! Read on—more reasons and evidence follow.

4

Female Body Exposed

As we have shown, males are not responsible for their bodily responses to the sexual display that females provide. In contrast, females can choose what they wear and looking sexy is in style. We repeat, whereas *sexy* to a man means SEX; *sexy* to a woman means many things, typically looking great or attractive as a person. Females have been enticed into exposing their bodies through the fashion industry and the media. For example, GNC (General Nutrition Centers) promotes many products and sponsors many ads claiming: "Healthy is the New Sexy." A recent book is also titled *Healthy is the New Sexy*.[1] A female being healthy may mean being sexy to her, but likely means SEX to a male if she reveals well-developed breasts, buttocks, and legs.

Female Figure

Not all female figures are voluptuous, that is, "curvaceous and sexually attractive"[2] and being "attractive and curvy."[3] One definition says: "Curvy refers to a waist-hip differential of .75." It is sometimes referred to as an "hourglass figure" when the female is not fat.[4] Tight clothing, such as form-fitting skirts, blouses, and pants,

51

can reveal a voluptuous body. Those females with voluptuous figures who show them off with what they wear are guilty of harassing moral males. Magazines, movies, and all forms of media are filled with female figures that are most often hourglass, curvaceous, and voluptuous. They are open displays of harassment against moral males.

Female Body Types

Four traditional female body types described by the fashion industry are Apple (inverted triangle with larger upper torso), Banana or Straight (rectangular, less difference between the waist and the upper or lower torso), Pear (upward triangle with the lower torso larger than the upper), and Hourglass (points of both triangles meeting at the waist with upper and lower torso almost equal in size, i.e., 36-26-36). Wikipedia says:

> The hourglass figure is perhaps the most iconic of the four major body shapes, as reflected by the fashion industry. Such fashion designers as Christian Dior have designed clothes with the female hourglass body shape in mind. Fashion designers of today continue to design clothes to fit the hourglass body shape even though the body shapes of modern women are changing and becoming much more varied.... Research conducted in Britain by the University College London and the London College of Fashion found that less than 10% of women had an hourglass body shape. The smooth and narrow waist continues to dominate in fashion designs meant to cater to plus-size women even when that particular body shape, the hourglass, is not commonly found.[5]

There are variations of the four traditional female body shapes, but body fat or lack thereof (fat or skinny) and clothing will make a difference in how voluptuous a female looks, regardless of body type. Some females begin with a sexy advantage if they have an hourglass figure. The size and curvaceousness of both the breasts and buttocks will register significantly on the visual reflexes of men, resulting in a strong struggle for the moral males and a need for them to look away to maintain their desire not to be sexually stimulated and thereby harassed.

Although there are many ways a female can make herself sexy, we are limiting ourselves to only a few of them. For example, there are bodily movements, voice modulation, facial expression, and so forth that can be sexually erotic. However, we have restricted ourselves to the few that are the top tempters for the males when they see them.

Breasts

Testosterone drives what is called the "Man Trance," which is described as the "glazed-eye look a guy gets when he sees something sexually appealing."[6] It is the look a man gets, especially when he sees breasts and indulges in the view. The breasts are the top female body part that leads the parade in the panorama of sexual instigation of sexual harassment of moral males. The female breasts can be provocative even when covered and sometimes more so when partially covered. Females with noticeable breasts, even when fully covered, will prompt the eyes of males as they know what's underneath and can imagine what is not seen.

Females with breasts that are partially covered, show-ing cleavage, can be even more distracting for males as they act as a tease or a come-on, especially when the nip-ples are almost showing. Male eyes will see only what is partially there, realize the rest, and thereby stimulate the automatic and involuntary sexual response. For some Jews, Christians, Moslems, and certain other religions, revealed cleavage is considered taboo.

Low-cut blouses, low-cut dresses, tight blouses, sheer blouses, T-shirts, V-neck blouses and dresses are all clothing that can accentuate female breasts and cause them to be a distraction for those males who prefer not to be sexually stimulated by them. Simply put, the more prominent the female breasts, the greater the likelihood they will be a source of genital stimulation for a male and thus serve as harassment for moral males. Also, the more cleavage of the breasts and the larger the breast size a female has, the more probable will be the resulting sexual harassment.

Adding to and compounding the possible sexual harassment attire are the camisole, tank tops, halters, and swimming suit bras, as more female skin is show-ing, along with a possibly provocative breast size and the amount of cleavage revealed. Female breasts can be easily displayed by women at any time during the sea-sonal year, depending on the style of clothing the woman chooses and how much skin she decides to reveal.

Not everyone agrees on how much exposure is ac-ceptable. Such disagreement easily arises when people live by different standards. Devon Franklin and his wife, Meagan Good, and an audience member illustrated this polarization of standards at a church event. Franklin is a Hollywood producer, best-selling author, preacher, and motivational speaker. Good is an actress who has appeared in numerous television shows, films, and music videos. Good and Franklin were featured at a church event promoting their book titled *The Wait*. During their presentation an audience member questioned Good about the low-cut gown she had worn at a previously held celebrity event. The audience member said:

> You are beautiful. I'm gonna say something to you. No, no, no, no, this is not offensive, but I was at the grocery store, and I looked at a newsstand, and I saw you, and you had your breasts showing.... So I wasn't going to come here, but the Lord brought me here to see you.... You have to make sure what you say and what you do match up. So we cover up, right?

Good's husband came to her defense and firmly declared, "She is not going to cover up. She will wear what she wants to wear in the name of Jesus. Amen. Yes, she will."[7]

Buttocks

The second, most stimulating body part, which can have a large impact on male genitals, is the female posterior. Wikipedia reports: "In humans, females generally have more round and voluptuous buttocks, caused by estrogen that encourages the body to store fat in the buttocks, hips, and thighs."[8] Aside from the possibilities at the beach, female buttocks are not normally subject to cleavage fashions as with the female breasts. However, with leggings and other tight or form-fitting clothing, the voluptuousness of the female buttocks of the right size and dimension, especially with cleavage (though covered), will have a dramatic and sexually stimulating and therefore harassing effect on moral males. Depending upon how voluptuous they are, the more cleavage of the female buttocks, the greater the resultant reflexive response by the male genitalia. Nevertheless, females are generally not even aware of the male attention they draw when bending over with their buttocks in male view, as they innocently open a file drawer at work or bend over to pick up a dropped object. Neither do they realize that such generally innocent actions can be a way to stimulate a male's genitals and thereby harass moral males.

Short skirts, short dresses, shorts, and tight or form-fitting clothing of many kinds are potentially sexual dynamite for males, which moral males must resist to avoid incendiary possibilities that can sneak up on them unawares and cause a genital response. Combine a female's voluptuous buttocks with her voluptuous breasts and it is double dynamite for explosive male sexual arousal and sexual harassment of moral males.

Female Legs

Shapely legs are an indicator of fitness, and, when they are bare, female legs are sexually arousing and harassing for moral males. Women's legs are treated as sexy in the media and in the culture. Women shave their legs to make them smooth and appealing. Short skirts and slit dresses act as teasers as to what lies underneath, and where the legs lead. They will subtly ignite the male imagination, resulting in sexual harassment for moral men, who do want to even think such thoughts. Female legs clothed in tights, leggings, and other form-fitting pants that show the shape of the legs can also be provocative depending upon the shapeliness of the legs.

High Heels

High heels and especially spike heels emphasize the shapeliness of the legs and serve to exaggerate the buttocks and breasts. They can make a woman look very sexy as she struts along adjusting her posture to accommodate the high heels. One survey revealed that 72 percent of women wear high heels some of the time and 28 percent of women never wear high heels.[9] They are definitely not worn for comfort or health. They are worn for style and how they make a woman feel—stylish and sexy.

Depending upon what else females may be doing to make themselves look attractive and sexy, high heels can add to the appeal. The higher the heels, the more the breasts are pushed forward and the buttocks are pushed back and up and the more voluptuous they will appear. They will be more prominent and unavoidable to the male eye. As high heels enhance the breasts and buttocks, they draw men's eyes to their sexy appeal. Thus, high heels, along with other bodily enhancements, add to the potential harassment of moral men.

High heels are one accoutrement of sexy dress that women should discontinue for their own good. Not only would that reduce the sexual harassment of moral males, but it could also prevent future physical problems caused by wearing shoes that harm the feet and throw the body out of alignment. As one author reveals, there is a long-term cost in strutting or stumbling around in high heels.

After describing research on the sexual attractiveness of high heels, he says:

> But this increased desirability comes at significant cost: High heels are uncomfortable and substantially increase risk of foot soreness, blisters, bunions, falls, ankle sprains, plantar fasciitis, ingrown toenails, nerve damage in the feet and legs, and knee and back pain.[10]

Ending the high heel era would be a classic win-win situation where the moral males would be relieved of the potential sexual harassment and the women would obtain physical health benefits.

Female Skin

The bare female body skin, whether at the beach or elsewhere, can be a sexual attraction and sexual distraction for a moral man, who would rather not look. The female legs have the greatest amount of skin available to be nude with the buttocks next and finally the breasts. The display of unclothed female legs is most common at the beach, but can be seen elsewhere, particularly in warm weather.

Those numerous females in America who dress in sexually provative ways need to own up to the fact that they are harassing moral males. If all females would stop the provocative dressing, males would no longer be harassed. To stop the sexual harassment against moral males, females especially need to keep in mind their three sexually stimulating body parts if they would not be guilty as charged. **Taking care of the breasts, buttocks, and legs, by reducing the amount of skin**

showing and shape revealing, will go a long way to ease the harassment of moral males.

Femme Fatale

A *femme fatale* is "an alluring and seductive woman, especially one who leads men into compromising and dangerous situations."[11] Those moral males who feel harassed by sexy females know that such females can naively or knowingly tempt them to compromise their integrity. Sexy females are the ones who are harassing moral males, who do not want to be enticed into compromising situations.

5

Sexual Objectification

Central to the subject of *S.H.A.M.E!* and key to exposing the source of the sexual harassment is sexual objectification, which is a combination of sexualization of women and the subsequent objectification of them. As we use the expression "sexual objectification," we are referring to the act of treating females solely or primarily as objects of male sexual desires, rather than as whole persons—fellow human beings.

Sexy body displays lead men to objectify females and, therefore, fail to see them as whole persons. The result of all the studies on the male brain and exposure to erotic stimuli, such as a sexy-looking woman (described in Chapter 3), is to instantly activate the parts of the brain related to getting an erection. This immediate communication from the male's eyes to his brain and his genitals leads to objectifying sexy-looking females. As we previously said, male brains are hard-wired to see sexy females as sex objects. Therefore, when females make themselves look sexy, males will objectify them. All females need to be aware of a certain formula, which is this: the sexier you look, the more a male will objectify you.

Not only do men see sexy-looking women as objects; they visually dissect them into separate body parts, particularly the sexually appealing ones. According to *LiveScience*, the "Brain Sees Men as Whole, Women as Parts."

> A glimpse at the magazine rack in any supermarket checkout line will tell you that women are frequently the focus of sexual objectification. Now, new research finds that the brain actually processes images of women differently than those of men, contributing to this trend.

> Women are more likely to be picked apart by the brain and seen as parts rather than a whole, according to research published online June 29 in the *European Journal of Social Psychology*. Men, on the other hand, are processed as a whole rather than the sum of their parts.

> "Everyday, ordinary women are being reduced to their sexual body parts," said study author Sarah Gervais, a psychologist at the University of Nebraska, Lincoln. "This isn't just something that supermodels or porn stars have to deal with."[1]

The Male Gaze

When females sexually display their bodies, men will be inclined to gaze at them as sex objects. Chapter 4, "Female Body Exposed," refers to the "Man Trance." An important similar element in male-female relationships is called "the male gaze":

The "male gaze" invokes the sexual politics of the gaze and suggests a sexualised way of looking that empowers men and objectifies women. In the male gaze, woman is visually positioned as an "object" of heterosexual male desire. Her feelings, thoughts and her own sexual drives are less important than her being "framed" by male desire.[2]

The media has capitalized on the "man trance" and the "male gaze," and women have been the losers. As females expose their bodies in sexually erotic ways that attract and engage the "man trance" or the "male gaze," they are placing themselves in a one-down position in relation to their male viewers, who from a one-up position are drawn to objectify them. The sexy look triggers the man trance, the male gaze, and the sexual objectification that follows.

The indulgers, who look to their heart's content, are male gazers. They are the ones who, with a short or long lingering look, are salivating after the flesh of those female bodies. The sexy-looking female becomes the one-down person as she elevates the indulger-male-gazers into the one-up position by quenching their sexual appetites. Even as some females may feel a sense of power in being able to attract males with their sexy-looking bodies, such power relies on the response of the male as judge. Such power is deceptive, because such females are turning themselves into objects and even merchandise.

Ogling Attraction

As females have fallen for the sexy look, either naively or knowingly, they have made themselves sexual
objects in male eyes. They have fallen into the trap of
sexualization. In Chapter 1 we use the following definition of the adjective *sexual*, which is "relating to instincts, physiological processes, and activities connected
with physical attraction." Additionally, we define *sexy*
as "Sexually suggestive or stimulating: erotic." *Sexy* can
also mean "seductive." The verb *sexualize* means "make
sexual; attribute sex or a sex role to."[3] Thus the noun
sexualization would be "the act of sexualizing someone"
or "seeing someone in sexual terms,"[4] as in the sexualization of the female body.

Whether adjective, verb, or noun, the above terms
are usually pejorative when they are used to describe
their use in revealing the media's ubiquitous influence
on women. Sexualization is thus linked to "sexual objectification." When a female is sexualized, she is objectified: seen and regarded as a sex object and evaluated in
terms of her physical characteristics. Thus, sexy-looking
females are naively or knowingly contributing to the
sexualization and objectification of females in general.
Rather than females being seen and evaluated according
to who they are as persons, they are evaluated by their
body shapes and bodily exposures.

The subject of sexual objectification is somewhat
like the adage: "We see things not as they are, but as we
are." Sexual objectification is instinctively in the eye of
the male, unless he suppresses it by diverting his eyes
and thoughts away from the visual scenery. Many female
and male writers have written extensively on this subject

from their personal points of view. We take the view of moral males who do not want to evaluate women according to their sexual display. In fact, they are offended and feel harassed by those females who naively or knowingly make themselves sex objects, thereby inviting sexual objectification.

Beauty Pageants and Dog Shows

Our concern is about all those places where males who desire otherwise are forced to see sexy females to their own personal detriment. These possibilities exist in every media form and in all publicly available places where women's bodies are being exposed, evaluated, and judged, such as beauty contests like Miss Universe, Miss World, Miss International, and Miss Earth. Also, on the local level there is the Best Bikini Competition. While those who would rather not see too much female flesh publicly exposed would not go to such events, the media covers such happenings as they are interspersed amidst the news.

Two different aspects of dog shows can illustrate the difference in how something is viewed. Most people think of dog shows as dogs being judged and evaluated according to breed, looks, and stance. This is all external and based upon the structure of the parts. The other kind of dog show involves the evaluation based on obedience, training, and tricks the different dogs can perform. Yet, even this does not even touch the personality of the dog as a family pet. How much more tragic is this when female human beings are put on display for their sexual attraction or put their own sexy bodies on display.

When sexual objectification occurs, females are identified by their body parts or sexual function and therefore lose their identity of body, mind, and soul/spirit. Sexy-looking females then provide visual enjoyment to indulgers as sex objects. Females baring their body parts are inviting sexual objectification to their own undoing. The more females provocatively expose their individual body parts, the less males will see them as whole persons with various virtuous, compassionate, and intellectual qualities that a male can admire and appreciate. The moral males who are harassed by sexual display are opposed to the degrading of females into the status of objects, simply or primarily designed for sexual pleasure. On the other hand, indulgers freely and frequently objectify females and degrade them in the process.

Feminist Perspectives

"Feminist Perspectives on Objectification" is a comprehensive publication, maintained by Stanford University, on the various feminist views on the subject of sexual objectification. The beginning of the paper says, "Objectification is a notion central to feminist theory. It can be roughly defined as the seeing and/or treating a person, usually a woman, *as an object*." Following this introductory statement is a list of ten features "that are involved in the idea of treating a person as an object." Two of the features are: "*reduction to body*: the treatment of a person as identified with their body, or body parts" and "r*eduction to appearance*: the treatment of a person primarily in terms of how they look, or how they appear to the senses."[5]

The statement that follows the list of features is an essential ingredient regarding how different people view sexual objectification:

> The majority of the thinkers discussing objectification have taken it to be a **morally problematic phenomenon**. This is particularly the case in feminist discussions of pornography.[6] (Emphasis added.)

Because of their many objections to sexual objectification we name those feminists "moral feminists" in this regard.

Contrary to moral feminist concerns regarding sexual objectification, one section of the paper considers "the possibility of positive objectification" and says, "A number of thinkers, however, have challenged the idea that objectification is always morally problematic." These feminists claim that it is wrong to "anthropomorphise humans and consider them more than they are." Such feminists contend that: "In the case of pornography, then, there is nothing wrong... with treating pornographic actors and models as objects for sexual pleasure and deny their humanity."[7]

We contend that it is morally wrong for those few feminists to justify the sexual objectification of females, particularly when they give strong approval to females selling their bodies as prostitutes and/or for male pornographic pleasure. Pornography has ruined many males and their families by ramping up the lust for sexual gratification. Such behavior only pushes sexual objectification of females, which demeans the female gender and harasses males who are morally offended.

Media Sexualization

The American Psychological Association Task Force on Sexualization clearly states:

> Virtually every media form studied provides ample evidence of the sexualization of women, including television, music videos, music lyrics, movies, magazines, sports media, video games, the Internet and advertising.[8]

We will now give examples from the above list that reveal the systemic sexualization of females:

Television

"Percentage of characters in family films wearing sexy attire by gender: 28.3% women, 8% men."[9] According to an extensive report titled "The Sexualization of Girls: An Update":

> Television Studies in the U.S. and other developed nations have shown that upward of 75% of television programming contains sexual content (Al-Sayed & Gunter, 2012; Eyal, Raz, & Levi, 2014). Sexual content may not be as problematic as sexualizing content (that is, the portrayal of women as sexual objects). Portrayals of women in television as sexually objectified occurs in 45–50% of cases, and these portrayals include body exposure that reflects cultural standards of beauty and thinness (Flynn et al., 2015; Smith, Choueiti, Prescott, & Pieper, 2012). In recent research on sexualization in children's TV programs, McDade-Montez, Wallander, and Cameron (2017) randomly sampled 32 episodes of 10

top programs (averaging 3 episodes per program) identified by white and Latina girls. Sexualizing content was present on an average of 24 incidents per program. Every episode had sexualizing content, 72% targeting female characters. White characters were sexualized more than Latina characters with regard to wearing heavy makeup or wearing sexualized clothing; but Latina characters were represented more in the categories of "wearing high heels" and "wearing revealing clothing." Some severe forms of sexualization that were looked for were not found (e.g., sexual aggression). But the coders did find in children's programing sexist comments, sexual harassment, attempts at manipulating a person into a romantic relationship, and unwanted sexual touching.[10]

Music Videos and Lyrics

An article titled "Female artists increasingly portrayed with sexually suggestive movements in popular music videos" reviewed the following findings of a study done at the University of Vienna:

> "Given that today's mainstream media (e.g., television, print materials, video games, social networking sites) are marked by depictions where sexual appearance, physical beauty, and sexual appeal to others are emphasized, both experts and members of the general public have called attention to this omnipresence of sexualization in mass media," said study author....

"A central finding of our study is that depicted sexuality and sexual objectification in music videos have been and continue to be pervasive in mainstream music culture. More importantly, our findings suggest that depictions of ambiguous sexual expression did increase over time."[11]

In their document titled "Sexualization of Popular Music," Division 46 Task Force of the American Psychological Association reports:

Research has found that exposure to sexualized music is related to self-objectification among adolescent girls, which is then related to the development of beauty ideals, body surveillance, body esteem, dieting patterns, anxiety levels, and mathematical performance.[12]

The APA Task force further noted that sexualized music combined with video performance leads to the girls "feeling less attractive, having less confidence, lower levels of body satisfaction." Along with the harmful sexual objectification of females comes research that reveals that "exposure to sexualized music is associated with risky sexual behavior." Indeed, when females are objectified in their own minds, they are more vulnerable to exploitation; and, when males objectify females, they are more likely to sexually pursue her as an object for sexual gratification.

Movies

Movies have been strong purveyors of the sexual objectification of women ever since the beginning of silent movies: from Jean Harlow to Marilyn Monroe and onward. A study, "commissioned by the Geena Davis Institute on Gender in Media and funded in part by the United Nations, examined films for their number of female characters, the roles these women played, how they were sexualized, and the gender of the filmmakers." Stacy Smith, the study's lead researcher said that they "monitor the one hundred top-grossing [U.S.] films each year, so this was a chance to examine what popular films look like in other territories." The following is some of what they found:

> More than just discrimination in their employment, female characters were constantly fielding comments about their appearance. Remarks and reactions—"verbal/nonverbal utterances"—to looks or desirability were, globally, five times as likely to be targeted toward female characters than their male counterparts; as the researchers wrote, "No matter the territory, female characters cannot escape an emphasis on appearance."

> The team further surveyed the levels of revealing clothing, nudity, thinness, and implications of attractiveness for female characters across age groups. For example, in the German films, 40 percent of all female characters wore revealing clothing (defined as "tight and alluring"). In American films, for comparison, 29 percent of the female characters were scantily clad. And in perhaps the most disturbing finding, teenage girls as young as 13 were as likely to be sexualized as women in their thirties.

Smith, though, didn't find this all too surprising. "These are entrenched trends that we see very consistently from year to year in U.S. films," she said. Only when characters passed the 40-year-old benchmark were they less likely to be sexualized.[13]

Movies not only reflect the culture but highly influence it. As viewers get used to seeing women sexualized in movies, they become used to it and are ready for more sexual objectification of women. Women readily cooperate because they want the roles and will compromise if necessary. They will dress and behave however the director wants the role to be played. Moreover, they are then admired for their sexy looks and may fail to realize that they are presenting themselves as sex objects, thereby demeaning themselves and setting forth examples for others who would like to be admired as well.

Magazines

Magazines have been a hot seller of sex with numerous photos of erotic-looking women, clad in a bikini or less up to just enough of the breast showing to lure the eyes and the imagination. Not counting the numerous porn magazines, a man can spend quite some time browsing through magazines to stimulate sexual pleasure. The problem for the harassed males who are bothered by such sexual exploitation of women is that such photos also appear in magazines least suspected. If not in illustrations with articles, they blaze forth from the ads that rely on the old saying, "Sex Sells."

Some of the magazines that sexually objectify women are actually women's magazines, such as *Cos-*

mopolitan, Vogue, and *Women's Health.* Although men may not read these magazines, women are influenced to make themselves appear as beautiful and attractive according to the latest trends illustrated directly on covers and content, as well as in ads. Thus, they are sucked into sexually objectifying themselves. Moreover, they then compare themselves with the so-called perfect bodies, enhanced and trimmed through photographic touch-ups, and never quite measure up.

Stephanie Murray, in her article "Are 'Sexy' Magazine Covers Empowering For Women?" says "This Evidence Says No Apparently sexualized media is bad for our mental health, and here's why I'm not surprised." She points out the prevalence and how the public is simply used to female exposure and the accompanying objectification. After referring to a couple of magazine covers, one being a cover on the *Women's Health* magazine with an actress "posing topless, with only her arms covering her bare chest," she says:

> To be honest, I can't say these covers surprise me. Nude photos of successful women make frequent appearances in the media. *Women's Health,* along with *Cosmopolitan, Sports Illustrated, Maxim,* and a slew of other popular magazines regularly feature sexually explicit content and imagery.

> Although nude images on magazine covers have lost their power to shock, they're still a relatively recent phenomenon. The degree to which women are sexualized in magazines, in song lyrics, on television, in video games, on the Internet,

in advertising, and in music videos today is unparalleled. As Dawn Hawkins, vice president of the National Center on Sexual Exploitation, describes it, "Yesterday's pornography is today's mainstream media."[14]

Although most men would probably not read these women's magazines, the covers are right out there for all to see, tantalizing ogling males, but harassing moral males, and demoralizing females.

Sports Media

Sports Illustrated covers are famous for their swimsuit contests, but in addition to sports magazines are the sexual objectification of female cheer leaders at the games. In fact, the Halftime entertainment gets more sexually provocative by the year. Not only that, but the female athletes are often admired by males more for their bodies than for their skill. Emily Liang, in her article, "The Media's Sexualization of Female Athletes: A Bad Call for the Modern Game," declares:

> One of the most important issues today is the **media's sexualization of female** athletes. Unlike male athletes, **female** athletes do not have the luxury of being primarily portrayed as performance athletes, as coverage of their beauty and sex appeal usually overshadow highlights of their on-field endeavors (emphasis in original).[15]

Video Games

Animated characters in video games often accentuate breasts and buttocks. This kind of depiction of the human body goes back to comic books such as *Wonder Woman*. The creator of the video does not have to find the perfect figure or enhance a photo. Each female is drawn to specification. Noelle Haslam, in her article "Miss-Leading Characters: The Hyper-Sexualization of Females in Video Games," declares:

> Although video games were originally designed to be a fun activity for everyone, the video game industry has been corrupted by marketing imperatives that target boys and men through the oversexualization and objectification of female video game characters. With gaming profits reaching nearly 140 billion annually, sex and violence have become cheap industrial ingredients. But at what social and cultural costs? In most video games, females in particular are often portrayed as hypersexual, submissive, and unintelligent. Sexualizing women in video games is how these companies make more profits.[16]

Here again, sex sells, to the detriment of all involved, as Haslam further states:

> The way in which women are modeled typically represents an ideal created by the hegemonic elite who control media production. This ideal is often spread across media to reduce women's self-esteem and encourage them to buy products that promise to increase their value. In most mediated content, including video games, women are encouraged to strive for hyper-feminine ideals and behaviors, while men are motivated to strive for hyper-masculine values and activities.

Within video games, female characters are shown with a slim figure, but large breasts and buttocks. Their facial features include seductive eyes with long eyelashes and colored plump lips. In contrast, men are depicted with a muscular body and wide shoulders. A chiseled jawline and generally broader features are common facial features.[17]

The Internet

The internet brings the world into the home for better or for worse. Although the internet supplies a wonderfully vast source of information, it is also a wide door into the sexual objectification of women, particularly through its vast underbelly of pornography and other forms of sexual exploitation that can adversely affect men and boys and women and girls. Sexual objectification of females appears without looking for it, as on the news channels and in the avalanche of ads. Every form of media shows up on the internet, so it is truly a combination of all the other media sources of hyper-sexualization right at one's fingertips.

A very personal and powerful tool for the sexual objectification of women is on social media, where females post selfies in various provocative poses. Such visual posts can generate many followers. Although the women may feel popular and admired through responses to their posts, they are actually reducing themselves to objects of sexual desire and pleasure. ScienceDirect posted an article from *Personality and Individual Differences*, titled "Picture this: Women's self-sexualization in photos on social media," which says:

> Wanting attention on social media was the strongest predictor of posting self-sexualized photos, and indeed, more sexualized photos garnered more likes on Instagram than less sexualized photos, and women who post more sexualized photos tend to get more likes in general and more friends/followers on both Instagram and Facebook.[18]

A study analyzing "600 Instagram posts from Four Year Party and College Nationwide" reveals one way that females are sexually objectified on social media. They say:

> The most reoccurring type of post across both sites highlights the attractiveness of a single female college student or a group of female college students. These are usually posted daily and show female students from a variety of colleges.... The women's names are not revealed and the focus of the post is their **sexualized body parts rather than their faces or smiles**.[19] (Bold added.)

These posts very blatantly reduce these nameless females to sexualized body parts as objects of lust. Perhaps the women feel protected by their anonymity. Nevertheless, what have they done to their personal identity? And, how many other females have felt safe to expose their bodies as objects of desire, as long as it's not face to face in real life instead of images on a screen?

Advertising

Why do advertisements for cars or any other products include a sexy woman? Again, sex sells! Paulina

Ezquerra hits the problem on its head in her article titled
"Modern ads continue to sexualize and objectify wom-
en." She says:

> Women have always been, and continue to be,
> sexualized in all forms of promotion, and these
> sorts of images are ubiquitous and normalized.

> No matter how much progress it feels like we've
> made, men — and the companies targeting the
> male demographic — continue to portray women
> as sexual objects, implying that male dominance
> over females is the most powerful advertising
> tool. Advertisements that degrade women to the
> level of the object they are attempting to sell fur-
> ther entrench our society with blatant rape cul-
> ture.

> This culture is one where the female body has
> been degraded to such an extent that our society
> accepts and normalizes the abusive sexualization
> of the female gender. This is done through ads
> that distract from a woman's humanity and ac-
> centuate her value as an object. [20]

The media draws eyes and particularly when female
sexuality is involved. As demonstrated above, the media
"provides ample evidence of the sexualization of wom-
en." It's almost impossible to avoid the media's ongoing
objectification of females and the harassment of moral
males.

Kathy Ireland

Highly successful role models for setting a high sexual objectification standard are those who achieve great popularity by the public display of their sexy bodies. Such individuals have set a high sexual objectification standard that has amplified the desires of females of all ages to follow. A prime example of this is Kathy Ireland, who "is a devout Christian." According to Wikipedia:

> Ireland was a supermodel in the 1980s and 1990s, best known for appearing in 13 consecutive *Sports Illustrated* swimsuit issues. In 1993, she founded a brand marketing company, kathy ireland Worldwide (kiWW), which has made her one of the wealthiest former models in the world. As a result of her career as a businesswoman, she had made a $420 million personal fortune by 2015.... During *Sports Illustrated* swimsuit's 50th Anniversary event, Ireland's 1989 cover was awarded "The Greatest Sports Illustrated Swimsuit Cover Of All Time" by its publisher.[21]

Ireland is to be complimented for her business acumen in achieving what she has accomplished. However, absent displaying her mostly unclad sexy body in 13 consecutive issues of *Sports Illustrated*, would she have become "one of the wealthiest former models in the world"? The lessons that many will learn from Ireland and other such females by their erotic modeling is that such bodily presence is to be admired and emulated as a means to attain popularity and possible fame and financial gain.

The moral females, including the moral feminists described earlier, would be critical of such displays that underscore the sexual objectification of females. The moral males we represent would be harassed wherever they may accidentally be confronted with such images in the media. While moral males can avoid purchasing *Sports Illustrated*, Ireland and other such erotic females are boldly within view through the media. Such provocative images may be difficult to avoid. Ireland and others like her promote the sexualization that is loved by the indulgers and resisted by the moral males. Moral males do not wish to compromise their integrity by looking at beckoning, bosomy babes like Ireland and others. They are harassed by such females who, like the Sirens of Greek mythology, lure males away from moral convictions and further promote the sexual objectification of their gender.

Sexualization is Pervasive

Everywhere a male turns, he is confronted with the sexualization of females, which can lead to the objectification of all females. The indulger enjoys all the visual food he can see to feed his sexual appetite, but the moral man must willfully resist taking it in. Therefore, he is being harassed by females revealing themselves in provocative ways that invite sexual objectification. Females should be offended as well, but instead, many join the ranks by following sexy fashion fads.

In summary, whenever females present themselves as sexy, they are objectifying themselves. When they compare their sexy parts with those of other women, they are also objectifying themselves and thereby reducing themselves to their parts. Some females capitalize on the sexual objectification as they find power in their sexual appeal. But the moral females, who want to be known for who they are, do not want to be reduced to their sexually appealing body parts. They would be aghast to think they are objectifying themselves for the sexual appetite of the indulgers and for the harassment of moral males, when they are just trying to look fashionably sexy. The offending women need to recognize and memorize these considerations and, thereby, syncretize what they wear with the results in the brains and bodies of males.

6

Sexual Harm Against Minors (By Women) Exposed

This S.H.A.M.E! acronym is the same as the title of this book, but in this chapter, it stands for Sexual **Harm** Against **Minors** (By Women) Exposed. The definition we use for the verb *harm* is "have an adverse effect on,"[1] where harm is inflicted on minors (girls and boys) in their development of identity, sexuality, and subsequent behavior. *Minors* are persons who are not yet adults. This includes both girls and boys. We use *By Women* to denote adult females. We will *expose* how this sexual harm against minors originates with women (adults) and results in **sexual harm against both girls and boys**.

During formative years attitudes towards identity and sexuality are being developed, particularly during their adolescence, when bodily and emotional feelings are being stimulated. As we demonstrate in Chapter 5, whether adjective, verb, or noun, the terms *sexual*, *sexy*, *sexualize*, and *sexualization* are usually pejorative when they are used to describe their use in revealing the media's ubiquitous and eventual influence on women and their subsequent influence on girls and boys. Here we emphasize the **harm** that women can inflict upon girls and boys simply by the way they dress.

Sexual harm against girls occurs when women (adults) sexualize them by setting themselves up as sexy examples to follow and also dressing them sexy as they grow up. Not only does a sexy-body image influence girls' attitudes about personal identity, but the sexy-body examples make them prone to sexually objectify themselves and thus be sexually objectified by men and boys. Girls are being set up to become sexualized as they grow up and sexually objectified by men and boys, as a result of sexy women in their environment (including mothers who strive to look young and sexy).

The sexy women are both harming and harassing the adolescent boys. They are harming them in the development of their attitudes towards SEX and the sexual objectification of females. They are directly harassing the adolescent boys with their own bodies and indirectly harassing them by setting a sexy example that girls emulate, which then adds to the harassing sexual exposure. The boys see many sexy girls, which prompts the same sexual response as men experience in response to sexy females (see Chapter 3). As testosterone fills the bodies of adolescent boys, they will become more and more aware of sexy breasts, buttocks, legs, and much skin showing on both women and girls.

The harm-harassment cycle feeds itself. All it needs is a few influential sexy females to get the cycle going. The girls follow the sexy-body examples of women and, in turn, harass the boys with their own sexy bodies. The girls sexually objectify themselves, present themselves as sex objects and are then sexually objectified by the boys. Many grow into adulthood with impaired attitudes about sexuality. This cycle of sexual harm is presently spinning at hypersonic speed. Will it ever stop? Who can put on the brakes?

Sexual Harm Against Females

We repeat the earlier quotation from the American Psychological Association (APA), which provides evidence for the sexualization of women, in which **they would include girls**. The APA states:

> Virtually every media form studied provides ample evidence of the sexualization of women, including television, music videos, music lyrics, movies, magazines, sports media, video games, the Internet and advertising.[2]

As we have shown in Chapter 5, pursuing all areas of the sexualization of women identified by the APA would reveal the same results.

More sexualization of the female body abounds today than ever before in this country. Understanding the sexualization of the female body is the key to understanding the public undressing of females. Sexualization of the female body with its accompanying undressing results in sexual harassment of men and boys and sexual harm to girls and boys. A great discrepancy of understanding between the sexes regarding what women view as sexy fuels the flames. In other words, the word *sexy*, meaning attractive, cute, stylish according to the female point of view, intensely shifts to SEX in the eyes of the male beholder. Therefore, females need to understand that what they purport to be a sexy body means SEX to males, and their genitals respond accordingly.

A multitude of examples throughout advertising reveal the outright, outrageous sexualization of women in this current cultural climate, which ultimately affects girls. Jean Kilbourne, who is in the National Women's Hall of Fame, began exploring the connection between advertising and several public health issues. Her DVD *Killing Us Softly 4: Advertising's Image of Women* is the latest version of her research and conclusions:

> This newest edition of Jean Kilbourne's influential and award-winning *Killing Us Softly* series shows how the advertising industry continues to reinforce, and glamorize, a regressive and debased notion of femininity. Using a wide range of contemporary print and television ads, Kilbourne lays bare the misogynistic [hatred of women] fantasy world of undernourished, oversexed, and objectified women, and examines these images against the real-world backdrop of eating disorders, men's violence against women, and the political backlash against feminism.[3]

One reviewer, Jennifer L. Pozner, Executive Director of Women in Media & News, says:

> In today's hypercommercialized media climate, Kilbourne's main point—that advertising creates

a toxic cultural environment in which sexual objectification, physical subjugation and intellectual trivialization of women has deep psychological and political resonance—is more compelling than ever.[4]

Another reviewer says:

Speaking before an appreciative audience, with accompanying visuals (advertising and print-media stills, television clips, and commercials) smoothly intercutting the lecture, Kilbourne clearly relays statistics, anecdotes, and quotes. Many of the clips show impossibly glamorous, thin women (sometimes digitally enhanced or a composite), and according to Kilbourne, girls and women often try to conform to these images, resulting in widespread eating disorders, low self-esteem, and depression. She believes some contemporary ads border on pornography, and females are objectified, and products (from burritos to beer) are sexualized.[5]

Sexual Harm Against Girls

Girls are growing up in an environment in which women are being sexualized and sexualizing themselves through provocative dress and are thereby being sexually objectified. In this kind of overly sexualized milieu girls will imitate sexually provocative dress from an innocent, naïve position just because they naturally want to look nice. Adolescent girls are highly vulnerable to becoming sexualized and thereby sexually objectified, both in their teens and as they grow into adulthood.

We quote from the "Executive Summary" of the "Report of the APA Task Force on the Sexualization of Girls":

> There are several components to sexualization, and these set it apart from healthy sexuality. Sexualization occurs when
>
> - a person's value comes only from his or her sexual appeal or behavior, to the exclusion of other characteristics;
>
> - a person is held to a standard that equates physical attractiveness (narrowly defined) with being sexy;
>
> - a person is sexually objectified — that is, made into a thing for others' sexual use, rather than seen as a person with the capacity for independent action and decision making; and/or
>
> - sexuality is inappropriately imposed upon a person.
>
> All four conditions need not be present; any one is an indication of sexualization. The fourth condition (the inappropriate imposition of sexuality) is especially relevant to children. Anyone (girls, boys, men, women) can be sexualized. But when children are imbued with adult sexuality, it is often imposed upon them rather than chosen by them. Self-motivated sexual exploration, on the other hand, is not sexualization by our definition,

nor is age-appropriate exposure to information about sexuality.[6]

The APA Task Force gives the following "Evidence for the sexualization of girls":

> Societal messages that contribute to the sexualization of girls come not only from media and merchandise but also through girls' interpersonal relationships (e.g., with parents, teachers, and peers). Parents may contribute to sexualization in a number of ways. For example, parents may convey the message that maintaining an attractive physical appearance is the most important goal for girls.... Research shows that teachers sometimes encourage girls to play at being sexualized adult women.... Both male and female peers have been found to contribute to the sexualization of girls — girls by policing each other to ensure conformance with standards of thinness and sexiness and boys sexually objectifying and harassing girls.
>
> If girls purchase (or ask their parents to purchase) products and clothes designed to make them look physically appealing and sexy, and if they style their identities after the sexy celebrities who populate their cultural landscape, they are, in effect, sexualizing themselves. Girls also sexualize themselves when they think of themselves in objectified terms. Psychological researchers have identified *self-objectification* as a key process whereby girls learn to think of and treat their own bodies as objects of others' desires.... In self-ob-

jectification, girls internalize an observer's perspective on their physical selves and learn to treat themselves as objects to be looked at and evaluated for their appearance.[7]

In their "Consequences of the sexualization of girls," the APA provides much research support for the following:

Psychology offers several theories to explain how the sexualization of girls and women could influence girls' well-being. Ample evidence testing these theories indicates that sexualization has negative effects in a variety of domains, including cognitive functioning, physical and mental health, sexuality and attitudes and beliefs.

Although most of these studies have been conducted on women in late adolescence (i.e., college age), findings are likely to generalize to younger adolescents and to girls, who may be even more strongly affected because their sense of self is still being formed.[8]

As the APA reveals, sexy female presentations are rampant throughout "virtually every media form" (see Chapter 5). The fashions presented in the media and promoted by the fashion industry emphasize the sexy look. Thus, a woman's desire for looking her best has been adulterated into having to look sexy and thereby wanting to look sexy. As females follow the fashions, they are simply copying what they see in "virtually every media" display and, thus, select clothing that reveals sexy attributes. The young girls are especially vulnerable as they are influenced by the media and by adult examples.

Almost simultaneously, the fashion industry presents sexy fashions for young girls and the girls soon reflect the fashionable examples of their adult female models.

Hollywood played a leading role early on in the undressing of females with all the sexy celebrity bodies on display. Hollywood has been a principle force of fashions throughout film history and a principle purveyor of sexualized females. Along with Hollywood, all the other visual and print media continue the sexualization that Hollywood began.

Social Media

Add the social media to the other media explosion and you have a 24/7 instrument of peer pressure. In her article "Social Media and the Sexualization of Adolescent Girls," Stephanie V. Ng, M.D., says:

> While concern about sexualization of adolescent girls is not new, social media has amplified age-old pressures for teenage girls to conform to certain sexualized narratives, as well as opened up new and uncharted ways for them to do so.

> Within a developmental period in which peer relationships are paramount and teens seek to differentiate between the "in group" and "out-group," social media is perfectly positioned to intensify and shape identity formation.[9]

An article titled "Media and Girls," which highlights the harm from media that sexually objectifies, stereotypes, and exploits girls for pleasure and profit, says:

The hypersexualization of very young girls, most notably in fashion and advertising, is a disturbing trend given that these stereotypes make up most of the representations of themselves which girls and women see in the media. The pressures on girls are exacerbated by the media's increasing tendency to portray very young girls in sexual ways. Over the past decade, the fashion industry has begun to use younger and younger models, and now commonly presents 12- and 13-year-old girls as if they were women....

The most cursory examination of media confirms that young girls are being bombarded with images of sexuality, often dominated by stereotypical portrayals of women and girls as powerless, passive victims... uniformly beautiful, obsessively thin and scantily dressed objects of male desire.[10]

Considering the examples of the sexual objectification of females in all the forms of media discussed in Chapter 5 and realizing how all that affects girls and boys should be a sobering wake-up call to all who care about the wellbeing and future of girls and boys.

Beauty Pageants

We give two extreme examples of the possibly innocent, but guilty mentality of many women regarding the depiction of the female body. The first is Jessica Simpson, a popular American singer, actress, fashion designer, and author, who featured a photo of her four-month-old daughter wearing a crocheted yellow bikini over her diaper.[11] The photo went viral and caused a war of words with some women outraged and others supportive. The second is Lindsay Jackson, who dressed her five-year-old daughter Madisyn Verst in a Dolly Parton outfit complete with padded breasts and padded buttocks for the *Toddlers & Tiaras* reality television show.[12] A brouhaha followed with polarized views bombarding each other.

The *Toddlers & Tiaras* reality show was about child beauty pageants, which generate controversy over dressing children provocatively and having them perform adult female "cute" sexy moves as they pose and sashay or strut across the stage. There are beauty pageants galore for all ages from toddlers to adults as these females vie against each other on the basis of their looks and how they display their beauty. These are not like once-a-year events. In fact, it is reported that Madisyn Verst had already won about 1,000 crowns by the time she was six-years old. These beauty pageants can be all consuming for the girls and their mothers.

Mothers, many of whom participated in beauty pageants, focus a tremendous amount of time and money on trying to make their own little girls more beautiful and even sexier than the other girls in the contest. They hire coaches for their little girls to teach them how to look, move, and pose in a cute, sexy manner that will most appeal to the judges. These mothers apparently believe they are building confidence in their girls and that they are thus preparing them to be successful in the future. But what they are actually accomplishing is a competitive attitude based upon looks, the most superficial aspects of personal identity. Moreover, all the attention given to a girl's appearance and the encouragement to show off engenders self-centeredness and a dangerously distorted view of what it means to be a girl.

Wikipedia describes the sexualization that occurs in these child beauty pageants:

> In preparation for these beauty pageants, children have their appearances altered by costumes, makeup, and other products which can objectify them at a very young age. Certain pageants encourage contestants to emulate grown women, applying heavy makeup to create full lips, long eyelashes, and flushed cheeks, wearing high heels and revealing "evening gowns," and doing provocative dance steps, poses or facial expressions. These things are not only preferred but expected if a child is to win the contest.
>
> The children participating in beauty contests may learn that they gain attention and status when being sexualized. The child perceives that sexuality is not only encouraged but can be a means to an end. This behavior can eventually lead to premature sexual activity and can teach an unfortunate lesson that a woman's worth is determined by their status as a sex object.
>
> "When you have them looking older, for a lot of people that means looking sexier. I don't think it's a great idea for girls at that age to be focused so much on their sexuality," Syd Brown, a youth psychologist practicing in Maryland told ABC News. "If you're telling a 6-year-old to act like a 16-year-old, you're telling her to be seductive and to be sexy."[13]

Beauty pageants for all ages involve judging the physical attributes of the female contestants. Other required attributes that may be involved, such as personality traits, intelligence, and talent, are not our concern, but rather the bodily exposure and emphasis. Presently most of the adult female competitions require every woman to display her body scantily clad in a swimsuit. The bikini was introduced as optional wear in 1946. Although it was banned from the Miss America contest in 1947, the 1951 winner of the Miss World contest wore a bikini. Pope Pius XII condemned the crowning as sinful. Thus, the bikini was banned from the Miss World contest until 1990. Later, the bikini again caused controversy, particularly when the pageants were held in countries with strong religious standards regarding modesty. In 2013, the bikini was banned again in the Miss World contest, in response to Indonesia's leading Muslim clerical body, which wanted the pageant to be canceled because of its "hedonism, materialism, and consumerism" and its "excuse to show women's body parts that should remain covered."[14]

Sexual Harm and Harassment Against Boys

Beginning in puberty and into adulthood the boy's brain is strongly sex ready. Images of breasts, buttocks, legs, and other female body parts normally capture male attention, and, for boys, this new attraction can increasingly come into focus until it occupies the center of their thinking. By the time a boy reaches high school, his testosterone has soared. Sex and body parts have been biologically pushed to the front of his awareness.

By then girls' body parts have developed such that these boys may even feel embarrassed about their interest in and even fixation on them. The boys, as well as the men, must exercise **thought suppression** to overcome the biological distraction caused by these sexy girls.

With all the opportunities to ogle girls and then women, some boys take to the readily available pornography even before adulthood. Girls who publicly parade around with clothing that emphasizes or reveals breasts, buttocks, and legs in provocative ways are feeding the adolescent boys' preoccupation with sex and female body parts. In doing so, such girls are contributing to the kind of over-exposure that, because of male hormonally-driven feelings being stimulated, can lead to a desire for more and more. Too many females are flashing their sexual assets at males from the adolescent years onward.

Girls need to recognize that, when they make themselves look sexy, they are sexually harassing boys. Many girls do this from their early teen (an even preteen) years by following the clothing styles promoted by adult women who proudly display their dazzling assets. Increased desire easily causes some male adolescents to become so preoccupied that they miss what is going on around them to the extent that schooling may suffer and family and other relationships may become burdensome. Moreover, the hyped-up desire may lead them to explore sexual activity with girls. In addition, females who flaunt their bodies are presenting distorted pictures of women to adolescent boys. Women and girls are more than sex objects, but boys can be distracted from believing that in light of the sexy visual evidence presented before their very eyes.

Sexual Harm Against Girls and Boys Ended

One powerful place to stop the sexualization of girls is the home. In spite of heavy peer pressure, parents can still influence their children. Both mothers and fathers can choose to model behavior that will help their girls resist becoming sexualized and thereby objectified. What mothers and fathers teach along the way, in addition to purposeful conversation, can be extremely important. For instance, when they are in view of females dressed provocatively, the parents can make a brief remark to discourage their daughter from emulating such dress, possibly by mentioning how the female is reducing herself into a sexual object and drawing the wrong kind of attention. An article entitled "Sexualization of Girls," reports on two studies related to what parents can do:

> In two studies, parental attitudes were examined with regard to sexualization of girls. Authoritative parenting style in mothers, including mothers who are less materialistic and mothers who are more religious, may help their daughters to be less affected by exposure to sexualizing material, or may prevent exposure (Starr & Ferguson, 2012). Parental monitoring of internet use is related to less harassment online (Khurana et al, 2015). Parental attitudes and direction are an unmined source of data that could be helpful in preventing the harm that may come from exposure to sexualizing media and marketing.[15]

Parents need to become involved. They need to educate their children themselves about sex and not leave it up to the schools and the media. The director of Culture Bound, an organization designed for "Building Resistance to Hypersexualized Media & Porn" in children through parental involvement, reveals: "Pornography has become the major form of sex ed for children."[16] Parents need to think about what they are doing and saying and what they need to do and say to save their children from the bondage of an overly sexualized culture. A question for sexy mothers of America: When you dress your daughters sexy, why are you surprised when boys are after them for SEX? A question for the fathers of America: Do you remember growing up and having thoughts about SEX when seeing sexy girls? Fathers need to man up to the need to accept their responsibility to help their girls refrain from sexualizing themselves in this overly sexualized culture. Fathers also need to help their sons through their moral example and through important conversations about sexuality.

In addition, all women are in a position to help end this sexual harm against girls and boys simply by dressing modestly. Those who are dressing in a sexy manner and thereby perpetrating the harm with their own naïve or knowing behavior can think about what they are doing and change for the sake of girls and boys. Sexy looking women need to recognize that, through the influence of the visual and print media, they are sexualizing their bodies and influencing girls to do the same. They may be the naïve mothers who influence their daughters according to the sexy fashions, indirectly through their own clothing and/or directly through dressing their daughters according to what is fashionably sexy.

Our culture is loaded with women and girls who have been sexualized and are therefore objectified as walking provocateurs that stimulate erections for boys, because their pre-adult testosterone levels automatically, spontaneously, and even unconsciously respond to voluptuous, sexy females (girls and adult women). By dressing modestly, the very women who are now harassing men and boys can leave the breeding grounds of sexualization from which the sexualization of girls originates. Former perpetrators of this sexualization of girls can make a big difference: by changing their own dress. By dressing modestly, they could help girls resist being sexualized by what they wear and thereby reduce the possibility of being sexually objectified by men and boys. **Along with parents who care about their children, nicely, but modestly dressed women can contribute much to end this horrendous harm to girls and boys.**

7

S.H.A.M.E!
Ended

Throughout this book we have attempted to expose—bring into plain sight—the sexual harassment against males by females. In Chapter 1 we describe the meaning of each word in the acronym S.H.A.M.E! to show forth what is hidden in plain sight and revealed in the remainder of the book. Chapter 2 is a brief history of the "Precursors of the Public Undressing of Females. Chapter 3 brings to light medical research regarding how and why males are genitally stimulated when confronted with sexy females. In Chapter 4, we show forth the primary female body parts that can produce provocative female appearances when exposed or exaggerated. The information we bring forth in Chapter 5, "Sexual Objectification," should be a prime reason for sexy females to correct their sexy ways to the benefit of both males and other females, as well as for their own good. Chapter 6 describes the sexual harm to girls and boys. We appeal to women, who are directly and/or indirectly encouraging girls to look sexy, to mend their ways and dress modestly. In this final chapter, we contrast the difference between a win-win-win-win situation for women, men, girls, and boys and a lose-lose-lose-lose dilemma for all women, which is in the hands of all sexy women to solve for their own good to the benefit of men, girls, and boys, as well as for other women.

We have documented the who, what, when, where, why, and how sexy-looking females sexually harass males and sexually harm girls and boys. The "who" are the sexy-looking females. The "what" is sexual harassment of males and sexual harm to girls and boys. The "when" is whenever a sexy-looking female dresses provocatively. The "where" is wherever the sexy female presents herself sensually. The "why" is to look attractive and to be physically admired by males and other females. The how is simply by dressing in such a manner that draws attention to their the breasts, buttocks, and/or legs by exposing and/or emphasizing these sexually stimulating female body parts.

Now that we have exposed the sexual harassment against moral men and sexual harm to minors by females and have revealed the fact that males have an instinctive, unconscious, spontaneous, and hard-wired response to sexy female bodies, we move to what needs to be done to counteract this harassment and harm. Once again, we use the acronym S.H.A.M.E! However, now the final letter **E** presents a new message: Sexual Harassment Against Males (By Females) **Ended!**

As we have medically demonstrated, sexy females who are provocatively clad will cause males who see them to be genitally stimulated. As such sensuous females come into view, males will be genetically aroused, unless they avoid looking or suppress the natural urge to look, which is sometimes impossible. These sexually provocative displays by females need to be **Ended**.

Win? Win? Win? Win?

All the medical and factual information in the prior chapters give solid reasons why the sexual harassment against males by females should be **Ended**. Among those reasons is the fact that ending the harassment by a move to modest dress for all females could be a win-win-win-win situation. A win for women, a win for men, a win for girls, and a win for boys.

Women

Ending the sexual harassment against men would be a win situation for women who want to relate to men as more than a sexual commodity. Sexual objectification of females ultimately demeans all women, encourages the indulgers, and offends moral men when they are forced to look.

The description of the Jewish *tznuit* in Chapter 1 is a good model to follow. In Chapter 4, "Female Body Exposed," we give several hot spots that will light up in the male brains and, therefore, their genitals. We assume that, with the Chapter 4 short list of suggestions, women who really care about whether males will view them as sex objects will follow that lead and strive to be attractive rather than being a sex attraction. They will dress modestly so that moral men will see them as friends and not as sex objects. That will be a big win for all females.

Men

Ending harassment against moral men would be a
win situation for those men who desire to relate to all
females as human beings of value: not only as mothers,
wives, and other family members, but also according
to their gifts and abilities: as thinkers, teachers, artists,
writers, scientists, medical practitioners, artisans, chefs,
farmers, and workers in whatever professions for which
they are individually suited. In other words, these are
men who do not want to be distracted by sexual display
that will possibly hide, mar, or distort the true value of
women and girls as individual persons.

We have heard women say, "All men are interested
in is sex." Our message to all such women is: you are
either greatly misinformed, travelling in the wrong company, or displaying a sexy-looking body. Throughout life
we have known or become acquainted with males near
and far—family, relatives, and many others. The variety
of men (religious or of no religious persuasion) that we
know want to view women as fellow human beings and
not as sex objects. Modest female dress is a win situation for men. When women dress modestly, these men
have the freedom to enjoy respectable conversations and
relationships without being distracted by enticing body
parts. That would be a big win for the moral men, and
perhaps an antidote for the indulgers.

Girls

Sexual harm of adolescent girls is a two-edged
sword: One: their sexual identity can be harmed; Two:
they may become sexual harassers themselves. Refraining from any sexual harassment against boys who want

to relate to them as people more than sex objects would be a big win for girls. Much of this depends upon significant role models of modest women. When girls and their female peers are daily barraged with media accentuating the sensual female body, they can naturally be enticed into thinking they must look sexy too. However, if mothers encourage attractive modesty by both word and example and if other women also dress modestly, girls will be enabled to resist both media and peer pressure and, thereby enjoy a win situation.

Such mothers and other moral females can make a dramatic difference in the lives of girls and young women. Girls especially need such encouragement as so many of them become obsessed with thinness and are constantly striving to reach some physical ideal that is unreachable. Not even the most physically attractive women look as good in real life as they are air-brushed to look in the media. Such distractions and obsessions with one's physical appearance can not only harm a girl's health; they can thwart her development in some of the most important areas of life.

The American Psychological Association's report on the harmful sexualization of girls describes when and where sexualization occurs. As mentioned in Chapter 6, in an environment of sexualization of females, girls begin to see themselves as objects in the eyes of others and their own identity gets wrapped up in how they look to others. As quoted earlier, "In self-objectification, girls internalize an observer's perspective on their physical selves and learn to treat themselves as objects to be looked at and evaluated for their appearance." The resulting negative effects of sexualization and objectification in girls' "cognitive functioning, physical and mental health, sexuality and attitudes and beliefs" can be horrendously harmful.[1] Therefore, all females, and particularly mothers, can and should think about what they can do to end the sexual harm to of girls. Women can turn the end of sexual harassment into a big win for girls.

Boys

As boys become adolescents, testosterone is filling their bodies and they become drastically aware of girls' bodies. Like men, boys become very alert to the various media's sexualization of females. Pictures of sexualized females will stimulate them, but another dramatic impact will be the girls, as well as women, in their immediate environment. To the detriment of both boys and themselves, girls are showing their breasts, buttocks, and legs more than ever before in U.S. history. The leggings style is in and the buttocks of girls register sexually in the bodies of adolescent boys, who immediately have a genital response. A win situation for the boys who desire to relate to girls as friends would begin with all women, particularly mothers, who dress modestly and teach their daughters about the facts of sexual objectification. Mothers setting a good example of modest dress and their daughters dressing modestly would be a big win for the boys.

Lose? Lose? Lose? Lose?

Whether ending the sexual harassment against males (by females) will be a win-win-win-win situation or lose-lose-lose-lose situation depends upon two groups of females. The first and most obvious group is comprised of those females who are sexy on purpose. The other group is made up of those females who are naively sexy. These two groups are the target of *S.H.A.M.E!* and are the ones responsible for the sexual objectification of their own gender.

Will it be Win? Win? Win? Win? Or will it be Lose? Lose? Lose? Lose? for women, men, girls, and boys? The majority of **moral feminists**, as we described earlier, are those who believe that sexual objectification is a "morally problematic phenomenon." They understand and have elaborated on, in their many writings, the demeaning of the female gender and are opposed to females being portrayed or acting sexy for the pleasure of male onlookers. There is a minority of other feminists, however, who do support females engaging in pornography and/or prostitution. [2]

Sexy-on-Purpose Females

The choice is up to the females who are **purposely sexy**. These women are guilty of promoting sexual objectification. They need to recognize that they are pleasing the indulgers who treat them as sex objects to please their lustful propensities. The **indulgers** would desire to see females looking as sexy as possible so that they can genitally enjoy looking at them and perhaps sexually indulge themselves. Indulgers love the genital thrill of sexy females and some go to the beach to pleasure themselves. A sexy female is always a win for them. Purposefully sexy females also need to be aware that the very males who want to regard them as friends and not sex objects are blocked or distracted from doing so. The **moral females** understand completely the concerns of the **moral males**, sympathize with them, and desire to see their own gender change to modest wear. Please keep in mind: the closer you look like a street-walker looking for business, the more you will attract the indulgers, while moral males will avoid you as much as possible. The indulgers would love to see you females as undressed and sexy as possible to ogle and gaze, fantasize, and add you to their repertoire for future sexual self-indulgence. In such a scenario, sexy female bodies become objects of lust. If these females want to be regarded as persons and not sex objects, they need to make themselves look like persons and not sex objects.

The more voluptuous a female appears, the more intense the mind/body impression and the more indelible and long-lasting the image. When they are immodestly dressed, these females are the ones that moral males most want to avoid, and they are the ones who are least able to form respectful relationships with the moral males. The more sexually intense the female, the greater will be the needed effort for the moral male to suppress both thought and bodily activity.

These are the females wherever they appear—live or in the media—who are setting a standard for other women and girls to follow. They are the ones who are most responsible for the sexual objectification of the female gender. They need to be in touch with the damage they are doing not only to men and boys, but to the female gender, young and old. To use simple moral terms: these sexy females need to repent, reform, and join the moral females and moral feminists who understand what *S.H.A.M.E!* is all about and dress modestly, which will open the door for respect from those moral males who desire a possibility for personal relationships. Sexy females will then applaud and join our efforts to reform all sexy females for the good of their gender. Otherwise the consequences of continuing the sexy status quo will be a lose-lose-lose-lose dilemma for women, men, girls, and boys.

Naively Sexy Females

The **naively sexy females** are innocent until informed. In most cases, females are unaware of the sexual impact they can have on males when they dress in a voluptuous manner. We hope that these females will read this book and, together with the females who purposely flaunt their bodies, will repent and reform for the good of their gender. We specifically appeal to mothers to set a modest standard for their daughters—to protect them from the downside of girls' objectification and open them up to the upside of modestly. The downside is found in the mind/body problems outlined in the APA report cited earlier (Chapter 5). The upside of modesty includes boys who will be free to regard girls as friends.

If all the sexy-looking females do not change their clothing habits, they will continue a Lose! Lose! Lose! Lose! situation for women, men, girls, and boys. If the sexy-on-purpose females and the naively sexy females would follow a modest dress code, as described in Chapter 1, they would change the current Lose! Lose! Lose! Lose! dilemma into a remarkable Win! Win! Win! Win! situation for all.

S.H.A.M.E!

In summary, we remind readers that two things happen in males upon seeing an erotic-looking female. **First**, the image is naturally, instantly, instinctively, and unconsciously registered in his genitals, because the response to seeing a sexy female is immediately communicated **unconsciously** to a male's genitals. Men are not always aware of it beginning, but it is a daily, behind-the-scenes occurrence. **Second**, the sexy female image is **consciously** recorded in his brain, adding to the brain bank of those images which can come up later. Thus, the erotic females are double-jeopardizing moral males (body and brain) and, worse for themselves, they are regarded as sex objects, which occludes the possibility of mutual regard.

S.H.A.M.E! is an appeal to both the males and females. To males it is a reminder and/or revelation as to what happens to their minds (thinking) and bodies (genitals) when viewing a sexy female. To females who are mainly complicitous, but naïve participants in the sexual harassment of males, this book is meant to reveal what is really going on. They need to know about their incendiary bodily harassment of males that occurs if they present themselves as sexy bodies and then correct their public persona. Our goal is to impact the current state of the sexual objectification of females that is running rampant, from pillar to post, throughout society. We desire to have as many females as possible be seen as persons and not objects to please the indulgers, who are interested in sexy because they have their minds on SEX.

We encourage the moral males, moral females, and moral feminists to give us support for our modest effort to reach the mammoth goal of reversing the tidal wave of sexual objectification and lust fed by erotic-looking females. The sexual harassment of males by females will be difficult to change and will never fully disappear, but change can be partially accomplished by one female at a time. **This is a moral battle between the moral males, moral females, and moral feminists on one side and sexy females, who are supported by the entire network of every media form used to promote the sexual objectification of females on the other side.**

End Notes

Chapter 1: Sexual Harassment Against Males (By Females) Exposed

1   The word males refers to men and boys.

2   The word *females* refers to women and girls.

3   "Me Too Movement," https://en.wikipedia.org/wiki/Me_Too_movement.

4   "Sexual Harassment," Wikipedia, https://en.wikipedia.org/wiki/Sexual_harassment#.

5   "Sexual," Google *Dictionary* from *Oxford Dictionary*, 04-19-2020.

6   "Sexual Instinct," www.encyclopedia.com.

7   "Sexy," *Merriam-Webster*, www.merriam-webster.com/dictionary/sexy.

8   "Harassment Law and Legal Definition," definitions.uslegal.com.

9   *Ibid.*

10 "Exposed," *Dictionary*, google.com.

11 "Ultra-Orthodox Jewish Men Offered Blurry Glasses," *Santa Barbara, News-Press*, 8/11/2012. P. D6.

12 "Islamic clothing," https://en.wikipedia.org/wiki/Islamic_clothing, 4/13/2020.

13 "Tzniut," https://en.wikipedia.org/wiki/Tzniut, 4/13/2020.

14 Janet Ratloff, "Chemicals from plastics show effects in boys," *Science News*, Vol. 176, No. 13, p. 10.

15 "The Neural Roots of Intelligence," *Scientific American Mind*, Vol. 20, No. 6, p. 30.

16 Larry Cahill, "His Brain, Her Brain," *Scientific American*, Vol. 292, No. 5., p. 40.

17 *Scientific American Mind,* Vol. 21, No. 2, cover.

18 Christof Koch, "Regaining the Rainbow," *Scientific American Mind, ibid,* p. 16.

19 Deborah Tannen, "He Said, She Said," *Scientific American Mind, ibid,* p. 56.

20 *Santa Barbara News-Press*, Feb. 24, 2009, p. B5.

21 Scott Barry Kaufman, "Taking Sex Differences in Personality Seriously," Scientific American, 12/12/2019, https://www.real-clearscience.com/2019/12/19/taking_sex_differences_in_personality_seriously_288762.html.

22 Jan Donges, "You Are What You Say," *Scientific American Mind,* Vol. 20, No. 4, p. 14.

23 *Ibid.,* p. 15.

24 "Gender Differences," en.wikipedia.org/wiki/Gender_differences.

25 Cassandra Willyard, "Men: A growing minority?"American Psychological Association, https://www.apa.org/grad-psych/2011/01/cover-men.

Chapter 2: Precursors of the Public Undressing of Females

1 "Sexual Revolution," https://en.wikipedia.org, 2/8/20.

2 "Women's liberation movement," https://en.wikipedia.org/wiki/Women%27s_liberation_movement, 2/8/20.

3 Joyce Milton. *The Road to Malpsychia: Humanistic Psychology and Our Discontents.* San Francisco: Encounter Books, 2002, p. 8.

4 *Ibid.,* p. 9.

5 E. M. Thornton, *The Freudian Fallacy.* Garden City: The Dial Press, Doubleday and Company, 1984, p. ix.

6 *Ibid.,* p. 10.

7 Alison Lurie. *The Language of Clothes*. New York: Vintage Books, A Division of Random House, 1983, p. 3.

8   *Ibid.*, p. 212.

9   *Ibid.*, p. 213.

10   Ellen Melinkoff. *What We Wore: An Offbeat Social History of Women's Clothing, 1950 to 1980.* New York: William Morrow and Co., pp. 20-21.

11   "20 years ago today, the World Wide Web opened to the public," https://thenextweb.com/insider/2011/08/06/20-years-ago-today-the-world-wide-web-opened-to-the-public/.

12   "Male Gaze," Wikipedia, https://en.wikipedia.org/wiki/Male_gaze.

13   Ena Lencek and Gideon Bosker. *Making Waves:; Swimsuits and the Undressing of America.* San Francisco: Chronicle Books, 1989, p.

14   Richard Martin and Harold Koda. *Splash! A History of Swimwear.* New York: Rizzoli International Publications, Inc., 1990, p. 29.

15   "Why Sex Sells…More Than Ever," *Business News Daily*, 2/24/20, https://www.businessnewsdaily.com/2649-sex-sells-more.html

16   "Sexy," *Merriam-Webster*, www.merriam-webster.com/dictionary/sexy.

Chapter 3: The Eyes Have It

1   Biomed Central, "The Eyes Have It: Men Do See Things Differently to Women," *EurekAlert!* https://www.eurekalert.org/pub_releases/2012-09/bc-teh083112.php.

2   "It's All in the Eyes: Women and Men Really Do See Things Differently," *ScienceDaily News*, November 28, 2016, https://www.sciencedaily.com/releases/2016/11/161128121211.htm.

3   M. Bolmont, F. Bianchi-Demicheli, M. P. Boisgontier, B. Cheval, "The Woman's Body (Not the Man's One) Is Used to Evaluate Sexual Desire: An Eye-Tracking Study of Automatic Visual Attention," *The Journal of Sexual Medicine*, 2/16/2019, https://www.ncbi.nim.nih.gov.

4   "Hard-Wired," https://www.dictionary.com/browse/hardwired.

5   https://science.howstuffworks.com/life/inside-the-mind/hu-man-brain/brain8.htm.

6   "About Emotions," James Madison University, https://cse.google.com/cse?q=About+Emotions&cx=0164766677328605 19677%3Ah7le3e3by1g&ie=UTF-8

7   "Know Your Brain: Amygdala," *Neuroscientifically Challenged*, https://neuroscientificallychallenged.com/blog/know-your-brain-amygdala.

8   Ronald Virag, *Erection, The User's Guide*, Editions Clement, 2013, Kindle locations 354.

9   Charles Patrick Davis, "High and Low Testosterone Levels in Men," MedicineNet, https://www.medicinenet.com/high_and_low_testosterone_levels_in_men/views.htm.

10   "Instinct," Merriam-Webster, https://www.merriam-webster.com/dictionary/instinct.

11   Eric R. Pianka, "Can Human Instincts Be Controlled?" http://www.zo.utexas.edu/courses/Thoc/HumanInstincts.html.

12   "Instinctive," Oxford/Lexico Dictionary, https://www.lexico.com/en/definition/instinctive.

13   All the books that are scientifically credible provide the same information regarding the automatic, hard-wired response of the penis. However, we have not included some of the additional ones we read because they include examples with immoral sexual interludes, probably introduced by the publishers who believe that "sex sells."

14   Dr. Ronald Virag is described *in Erection, The User's Guide, op. cit.*, as a "French cardiovascular surgeon" who "specialized in andrology (the medicine of masculine health). Inventor of the first medical treatment for impotence, andrology, he designed many of the modern techniques of diagnosis and treatments for erectile dysfunction; and also a preventive program for effects of ageing in the cardiovascular, hormonal, sexual, urologic, and nutritional areas."

15   Virag, *op. cit.*, locations 320-323.

16   "Desire," Oxford/Lexico Dictionary, https://www.lexico.com/en/definition/desire.

17 "Reflex," Google from the *Oxford Dictionary*, https://www.google.com/search?client=firefox-b-1-d&q=reflex.

18 "Reflex," Wikipedia, https://en.wikipedia.org/wiki/Reflex, 4/13/2020.

19 "Reflex," Biology Online, https://www.biologyonline.com/dictionary/reflex.

20 Saskia Verhagen. *The Book of Erections: The Penis: A User's Guide*, https://www.numan.com/the-book-of-erections.

21 *Ibid.*

22 Shaunti Feldhahn. *For Women Only: What You Need to Know About the Inner Lives of Men*, Revised Ed. New York: Multnumah/Random House, 2004, 2019, p. 9.

23 *Ibid.*, p. 134.

24 *Ibid.*

25 *Ibid.*, p. 135.

26 *Ibid.*

27 *Ibid.*, p. 127.

28 *Ibid.*, p. 129.

29 "The legging problem," Letter to the Editor, *The Observer*, 3/25/2019, https://ndsmcobserver.com/2019/03/the-legging-problem/.

Chapter 4: Female Body Exposed

1 Terrence Robertson. *Healthy is the New Sexy: A Guide to Creating the Body You Want.* Germantown, MD: Best Seller Publications, 2019.

2 "Voluptuous," Google from the *Oxford Dictionary*, https://www.lexico.com/en/definition/voluptuous, 04-14-20.

3 "Voluptuous," Vocabulary.com, https://www.vocabulary.com/dictionary/voluptuous.

4 "Curvy," Leaf Group Limited, https://www.leaf.tv/articles/differences-between-plus-size-curvy/.

5　"Hourglass Figure," *Wikipedia*, https://en.wikipedia.org/wiki/Hourglass_figure, 4/15/2020.

6　"Man Trance," urbandictionary.com.

7　"Meagan Good told to 'cover up' during a church seminar," Fox News.com

8　"Cultural History of the Buttocks," *Wikipedia*, https://en.wikipedia.org/wiki/Cultural_history_of_the_buttocks.

9　"How High Heels Affect Your Body," http://www.thespinehealthinstitute.com/news-room/health-blog/how-high-heels-affect-your-body.

10　Michael Castleman, "The Uncanny Psychology of High Heels," *Psychology Today*, 12/13/2016, https://www.psychologytoday.com/us/blog/all-about-sex/201612/the-uncanny-psychology-high-heels.

11　"Femme fatale," Lexico/Oxford Dictionary, https://www.lexico.com/definition/femme_fatale.

Chapter 5: Sexual Objectification

1　Stephanie Pappas, "Brain Sees Men as Whole, Women as Parts," *LiveScience*, July 24, 2012, https://www.livescience.com/21806-brain-male-female-objectification.html.

2　Janice Loreck, "Explainer: what does the 'male gaze' mean, and what about a female gaze?" https://theconversation.com.

3　"Sexualize," Google *Dictionary* from *Oxford Dictionary*, https://www.google.com.

4　"Sexualization," *Cambridge Dictionary*, https://dictionary.cambridge.org/us/dictionary/english/sexualization.

5　*Stanford Encyclopedia of Philosophy*, "Feminist Perspectives on Objectification," Revised Version, 12/16/2019, https://plato.stanford.edu/entries/feminism-objectification/.

6　*Ibid.*

7　*Ibid.*

8   American Psychological Association, "Report of the APA Task Force on the Sexualization of Girls," https://www.apa.org/pi/women/programs/girls/report.

9   Asawin Suebsaeng and Dana Liebelson, "7 Ways Women and Girls Are Stereotyped, Sexualized, and Underrepresented on Screen," 11/30/2012, motherjones.com.

10   Sharon Lamb, Julie Koven, Charlotte Brown, Melanie Dusseault, Cara Forlizzi, and Lindsey White, "The Sexualization of Girls: An Update," Culture Reframed, https://www.culturereframed.org/wp-content/uploads/2019/01/CultureReframed-SexualizationOfGirlsReport-2019.pdf.

11   Eric w. Dolan, "Female artists increasingly portrayed with sexually suggestive movements in popular music videos," April 2019, PsyPost, https://www.psypost.org/2019/04/female-artists-increasingly-portrayed-with-sexually-suggestive-movements-in-popular-music-videos-53478.

12   American Psychological Association, "Report of the Division 46 Task Force on the Sexualization of Popular Music," 2018, https://www.apadivisions.org/division-46/publications/popular-music-sexualization.pdf.

13   Molly Mirhashem, "Study Discovers that Movies Sexualize 13-Year-Old Girls as Much as Women in Their 30s," 9/24/14, https://newrepublic.com/article/119562/gender-movie-study-film-industry-discriminates-against-women.

14   Stephanie Murray, "Are 'Sexy' Magazine Covers Empowering For Women?" 9/13/16, https://verilymag.com.

15   Emily Liang, "The Media's Sexualization of Female Athletes: A Bad Call for the Modern Game," Vol. 3, No.10, http://www.inquiriesjournal.com/articles/587/the-media-as-sexualization-of-female-athletes-a-bad-call-for-the-modern-game#:~:text=One%20of%20the%20most%20important,of%20their%20on%2Dfield%20endeavors.

16   Noelle Haslam, "Miss-Leading Characters: The Hyper-Sexualization of Females in Video Games," http://gcml.org/miss-leading-characters-the-hyper-sexualization-of-females-in-video-games/.

17   *Ibid.*

18 Laura L. Ramsey and Amber L. Horan, "Picture this: Women's self-sexualization in photos on social media," *Personality and Individual Differences*, Vol. 133, 10/15/2018, pp. 85-90, https://www.sciencedirect.com/science/article/abs/pii/S0191886917304129.

19 Stefanie E. Davis, "Objectification, Sexualization, and Misrepresentation: Social Media and the College Experience," *Social Media + Society*, 7/13/18, https://journals.sagepub.com/doi/full/10.1177/2056305118786727.

20 Paulina Ezquerra, "Modern ads continue to sexualize and objectify women," 4/3/2018.http://thedailycougar.com/2018/04/03/women-hypersexualized-ads/

21 "Kathy Ireland," Wikipedia, https://en.wikipedia.org/wiki/Kathy_Ireland, 07-17-2020.

Chapter 6: Sexual Harm Against Minors (By Females) Exposed

1   "Harm," Oxford Dictionary, https://www.lexico.com/en/definition/harm.

2   American Psychological Association. "Report of the APA Task Force on the Sexualization of Girls," https://www.apa.org/pi/women/programs/girls/report.

3   Jean Kilbourne. *Killing Us Softly 4: Advertising's Image of Women,* website description with reviews, http://www.killingussoftly4.org/.

4   *Ibid.*

5   *Booklist* review of *Killing Us Softly 4*, https://www.killingussoftly4.org/.

6   "Executive Summary," American Psychological Association. "Report of the APA Task Force on the Sexualization of Girls," op. cit. *Ibid.*

7   "Evidence for the sexualization of girls," *Ibid.*

8   "Consequences of the sexualization of girls," *Ibid.*

9   Stephanie V. Ng, "Social Media and the Sexualization of Adolescent Girls," *The American Journal of Psychiatry*, https://ajp.psychiatryonline.org/doi/10.1176/appi.ajp-rj.2016.111206.

10 "Media and Girls," reprinted from *Media Awareness* in "End the Sexualization of Girls and Young Women in Mainstream Media," *Challenge the Media*, https://www.theadvocatesforhumanrights.org/uploads/challenge_the_media_2.pdf.

11 Hollie McKay, "Jessica Simpson slammed for dressing four-month-old daughter Maxwell in bikini," Fox News, https://www.foxnews.com/entertainment/jessica-simpson-slammed-for-dressing-four-month-old-daughter-maxwell-in-bikini, 9/19/2020.

12 Hilary Levey Friedman, "Toddlers & Tiaras Justice," https://slate.com/human-interest/2012/08/toddlers-tiaras-custody-battle-should-maddy-versts-pageant-mom-be-punished.html, 8/31/2012.

13 "Child Beauty Pageant," Wikipedia, https://en.wikipedia.org/wiki/Child_beauty_pageant, 04/20/2020.

14 Harold Maass, "The controversial bikini ban at the Miss World beauty pageant," *The Week*, https://theweek.com/articles/463432/controversial-bikini-ban-miss-world-beauty-pageant, 6/7/2013.

15 Sharon Lamb, Julie Koven, Charlotte Brown, Melanie Dusseault, Cara Forlizzi, and Lindsey White, "The Sexualization of Girls: An Update," Culture Reframed, https://www.culturereframed.org/wp-content/uploads/2019/01/CultureReframed-SexualizationOfGirlsReport-2019.pdf.

16 "What You Need to Know About Kids & Porn: Culture Reframed," https://www.culturereframed.org.

Chapter 7: S.H.A.M.E! Ended

1   American Psychological Association. "Report of the APA Task Force on the Sexualization of Girls," https://www.apa.org/pi/women/programs/girls/repor

2   *Stanford Encyclopedia of Philosophy*, "Feminist Perspectives on Objectification," Revised Version, 12/16/2019, https://plato.stanford.edu/entries/feminism-objectification/.